LOOKING DOWN ON WAR

THE NORMANDY INVASION

DEDICATION

To Jack, Phil, Marv, Gil, Peter, Roy C., John, George, and Pete. Top notch USAF Intelligence professionals, old comrades-in-arms and treasured friends who achieved amazing things four and a half decades ago. In our day no one in the world could 'read out' a major photoreconnaissance mission faster or better. Some are gone but none forgotten.

LOOKING DOWN ON WAR

THE NORMANDY INVASION

Imagery from WWII Intelligence files

Colonel Roy M. Stanley II, USAF (ret.)

Pen & Sword
MILITARY

Other Books by the Author

World War II Photo Intelligence
Prelude To Pearl Harbor
To Fool A Glass Eye
Asia From Above
V-Weapons Hunt
Axis Warships

First published in Great Britain in 2012 by
PEN & SWORD MILITARY
an imprint of
Pen & Sword Books Ltd,
47 Church Street,
Barnsley, South Yorkshire
S70 2AS

ISBN 978 1 78159 056 0

A CIP record for this book is
available from the British Library.

Typeset by CHIC GRAPHICS

Printed and bound in India by Replika Press Pvt. Ltd.

Pen & Sword Books Ltd incorporates the Imprints of
Pen & Sword Aviation, Pen & Sword Family History, Pen & Sword Maritime, Pen & Sword Military, Pen & Sword Discovery, Wharncliffe Local History, Wharncliffe True Crime, Wharncliffe Transport, Pen & Sword Select, Pen & Sword Military Classics, Leo Cooper, The Praetorian Press, Remember When, Seaforth Publishing and Frontline Publishing.

For a complete list of Pen & Sword titles please contact
PEN & SWORD BOOKS LIMITED
47 Church Street, Barnsley, South Yorkshire, S70 2AS, England
E-mail: enquiries@pen-and-sword.co.uk
Website: www.pen-and-sword.co.uk

CONTENTS

ACKNOWLEDGEMENTS 6

FOREWORD 7

CHAPTER I   The Atlantic Wall 10

CHAPTER II   Aerial Photoreconnaissance 19

CHAPTER III   Understand the Defenses 52

CHAPTER IV   First In 63

CHAPTER V   Over the Beaches 89
                  Sword 91
                  Juno 106
                  Gold 124
                  Omaha 169
                  Ponte du Hoc 207
                  Utah 216

CHAPTER VI   Later and Inland 226

CHAPTER VII   Afterthoughts 254

MAPS 262

INDEX 269

ACKNOWLEDGEMENTS

A nod of appreciation to Pen & Sword's Brigadier Henry Wilson for seeing merit in the book, and to Matt Jones and Sylvia Menzies-Earl for putting up with my incessant changes while shepherding my seventh into print. A big tip of the hat to Susan Strange, independent researcher at the US National Archives Cartographic Branch, who has an exceptional talent for locating photos and documents. Gratitude to Chris Halsall and the folks at the Medmenham Archives for finding imagery I needed to fill in gaps. Thanks to Caroline Walsh and the BBC Interview Team for trading copies of images and ideas on the invasion. As always, a special thanks to my wife, Mary Ellen for putting up with photos strewn about the house, my long hours in research and writing, and demands for her excellent editing skills.

FOREWORD

If you've bought one of my earlier books (consider that a patriotic duty) you know my forte is photo interpretation (PI) of World War II aerial imagery, which I consider a major and underused primary source for understanding military history. My judgments and comments are based less on secondary sources than on imagery in my hands and my experience as a PI and Combat Intelligence Analyst. In this case I'm looking at the Normandy Invasion just as I would have any imagery-based study assigned when I was on active duty.

Preparing material for what I intended to be my seventh book I realized I had enough material for a separate book on the Normandy Invasion and changed direction.

You may ask what could I publish that would be new and different? The reader has likely seen some aerial views of the Normandy Invasion, but have you really SEEN them? It's been almost seven decades since the Normandy landings, how can I show you pictures of things you've never seen before?

I can because:

• Most historians don't have the skills necessary to find and understand what you'll see on these pages – particularly in my enlargements.
• Many of the recon photos in this book were collected when no one could be sure the Normandy Invasion would succeed, but by dark, certainly by mid-day on 7 June, troops were pushing inland expanding the beachheads and failure was no longer a possibility. On 6 and 7 June 1944 there was no incentive to expend scarce PI resources searching images of where the troops had been. PIs were searching farther inland to spot things the troops were going to encounter – and elsewhere to find the threatening V-1 launch locations springing up all over coastal France. So many of the images I've found were never selected and published, some possibly never looked at.
• PIs in 1944 didn't have the ability to easily enlarge and scan images like we can today using computers. Photographic enlargement was slow and inflexible, not good for 'trolling' through a mission, thus many of the images in my enlargements remained unseen. I didn't have computer enlargement capacity when I first found these photos so some of the images included here surprised me when I discovered them during research for this book using computer enlargement.

I don't pretend to know all the details of every event, piece of equipment or subject, nor do I think I've seen all of the available imagery, but I will interpret the imagery I've found for you. I think you'll find my USAF photo interpretation training and experience let me see a LOT more than most people writing conventional textual history. Most books on World War II use readily available and easily understood ground photos. Occasionally a book will show an aerial to prove a point or make the narrative more interesting—but without the benefit of photo interpretation. My books use imagery selected to tell the story. For me, text is an adjunct used to identify something, put it into context, or move the story along. In this book you will see well-known events from a different perspective. Don't think of this as a PowerPoint presentation or lecture series—think of it as the two of us sitting together in my library going through a stack of WW II prints, and I'm telling you what the photos say to me.

If you've got any of my earlier books you know how I discovered this imagery. As holders of DoD aerial film archives the unit I was in was under pressure to reduce cost of holdings, some of which had been dormant since the 1940s. Loath to destroy unknown material, I began a screening to see what we had. Missions I found from 6 or 7 June 1944 (and other dates I knew were significant) were sent to the U.S. National Archives to keep them safe. I've been told there was originally more aerial film but some was dumped in the ocean to save cost of shipping it back to America after the war. I've also been told by 'old timers', but couldn't confirm, that much of low altitude, oblique coverage was destroyed by the Cartography community (who were the first post-war recipients of the original roll film negatives) because it had no value for mapping.

I found only selected cut negative copies of British imagery. We assumed (hoped) all the original British-source material was in England.[1]

Clearly little of the designated material still had any Intelligence value in the 1980s but I began to find images I KNEW were historic and created over one hundred 30″ x 40″ display boards for our halls to create interest in the material. People cleared to enter our secure precincts were soon commenting favorably on photos of famous bombing raids, the building of the Pentagon, Pearl Harbor before 7 December 1941…and D-Day.[2]

When I collected these photos I had no thought of someday writing a book on the Normandy Invasion. I just knew the photos were important and interesting. Sorting what I had, assembling chapters for this book three decades later, I wish I'd looked harder and kept more − and used entire missions to plot locations of specific photos. I made heavy use of Google Earth maps to match fields and roads but you must bear with me when I can't always tell you a precise location. It also explains why some landing beaches have more coverage than others. It isn't because I consider any assault site lesser for any reason. It's simply because I didn't find, or didn't recognize, more material covering them.

Everyone has seen ground shots of the invasion. Those are individual photos, often unconnected in time and space. Aerial photoreconnaissance looks at war differently. PR aircraft take series of overlapping images. You often see the same ground on three or four consecutive frames. If you can recognize it, you can observe a place on different missions and analyze changes. From overhead, you see fixed and mobile targets that have been bombed (or attempted to be bombed). You see buildings destroyed by air or ground fire, usually accompanied by smoke. You'll see enemy strong points and tracks where armored vehicles have passed. If you're lucky sometimes PR lets you see the vehicles themselves. You sometimes see an actual explosion or fire, but photo recce immediately above and parallel to, the FEBA (Forward Edge of the Battle Area) is about the most risky thing a pilot can do − both sides are likely to shoot at the plane. Therefore it is extremely rare to see the instant of men crashing against a strong point or an anti-tank gun working its destruction, but you'll even see some of that in these pages.

The greatest advantage of PR over ground imagery is its scope − miles instead of feet. Aerial photos are invaluable in seeing an overall context of a situation or assessing capability

---

1. Later I was told, but couldn't confirm, that some RAF film had been destroyed in the 1960s because of its dangerously flammable nitrate base (USAAF used Safety Film after 1941).
2. Roll film could be pulled from the stacks for screening using date or location but the cut-negatives weren't indexed in any way so discovery of that material was completely random. Enthusiasm for the treasures I was finding encouraged me to write my first book in 1981 − and six others.

of an enemy force. You will see for yourself that aerial photos are also particularly effective tools for understanding the lines of communication and logistics of these events – the sheer weight pushing on shore in June 1944.

Note: To make reading easier, where possible vertical photos in this book are presented with north up. Obliques are shown as the camera pointed regardless of direction.

A final word on Photo Interpretation and Photo Interpreters. Three words are important. If a PI isn't sure, he says 'possible'. Pretty sure but not positive is 'probable'. If there is no caveat, it is highly likely something IS what he says it is (though I once read a report referring to 'probably a possible unidentified installation').

Chapter I

THE ATLANTIC WALL

Frederick the Great and Sun Tzu agreed that he who tries to defend everything defends nothing. But that's what Hitler tried to do in the West – from the Arctic Circle to the Spanish Border. Having taken that territory, he was loath to lose an inch of it, and rightly expected the growing force of Allied military strength would eventually try to return to the Continent. Commando raids in Norway and Dieppe, invasions in North Africa, Sicily and Italy itself convinced Hitler his fears were correct but didn't tell him where the invasion would come from the West. His response was to invest an enormous amount of energy, material and manpower in The Atlantic Wall. Probably the most pervasive impact of that decision was to place large numbers of troops in static positions, largely unable to support each other or form a decisive reserve in response to an invasion.

Hitler's propaganda machine churned out material designed to mollify the home folks while convincing the Allies that it was folly to attempt penetration of the 'wall'. Prior to 11 December 1942, that information reached America via Military Attachés in Berlin, Paris and Rome, and from British sources. After the U.S. declared war on Germany, information reached Intelligence files through Attachés in neutral nations and British sources.

The Nazis loved concrete. Typical was a much photographed massive casemate at Wissant, near Calais. Battery Todt (named for the Nazi engineering corps founded by Fritz Todt) was completed in late 1940 and housed four 380mm guns (15″). Situated at Cap-Gris-Nez, the guns were just 19 miles from Dover (within weapons range).

SCHWERE
BROCKEN
AM KANAL

A super heavy gun, probably 380mm, identified only as defending the 'Kanal', the German name for the English Channel. This magazine photo may show Battery Todt under construction near Wissant. Similar, if less spectacular, point defenses were being constructed all along 'The Wall', starting with ports, most likely landing places, and the most obvious or vulnerable targets. British Commando raids and Dieppe spurred emplacement of guns and, in some ways, steered German selection of sites to defend.

Intended to fend off invasion fleets, batteries featuring heavy guns were gradually extended along the coast to defend more of Nazi-held Europe. Work on the Atlantic Wall continued steadily throughout the war. Strong points, particularly heavy gun positions, weren't hard for PIs to find. Large disruptions of the earth and masses of concrete stand out as they break the normal patterns of the fields.

This is Noires Mottes, seven miles north of Battery Todt, 15 March 1943.

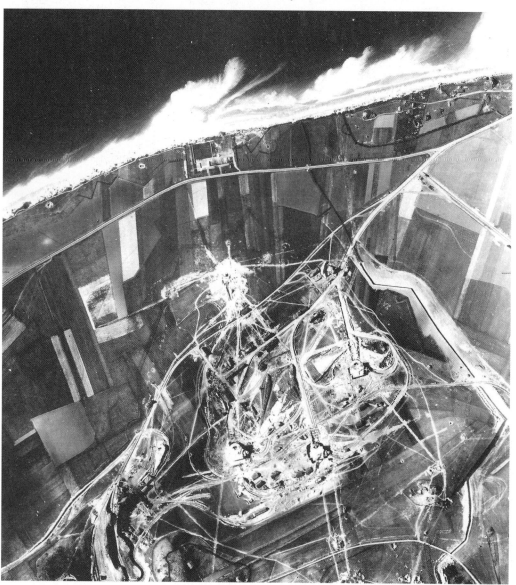

The three firing bunkers are nearly completed but not yet back-filled with a covering of earth. I don't see any barrels yet but Battery Lindemann eventually had three 16″ guns. A substantial anti-tank ditch is to the east and south. Apparently the defenders thought the most immediate threat was from an Allied landing near Calais.

Unten: **Die Wehrmacht übernimmt das Geschütz.** Die Bunker sind dem Erdboden angeglichen, das Fernkampfgeschütz selbst ist mit einem Tarnnetz überdacht, das den Einblick aus der Luft verwehrt. Die Wehrmacht hat das Geschütz übernommen, der erste Posten ist aufgestellt

A fold seam on the left shows this was probably collected from a German magazine by an American Attaché somewhere. Long-range guns like these were reserved for the most important locations, but there were a lot of field artillery guns and howitzers captured in Russia and France. Guns pulled out of older warships were used (sometimes in their original turrets), captured or damaged tanks provided lighter weapons (again sometimes still in the tank turrets). Smaller garrisons thus armed were steadily showing up in strong points creeping south from Norway and north and south of Calais. Positions with large guns (8″ to 12″) were built 'gun range' apart, one about every 20 miles in Normandy. Despite the German boast above, strong points were easy for Allied Intelligence to find on aerial imagery. Camouflage, as above, was mainly for show – aerial imagery in stereo looked right through the netting. Note the fake 'trees' on either side of the soldier.

When Field Marshal Erwin Rommel was put in charge of the Atlantic Wall he advocated repulsing an invasion on the beaches. That resulted in a flurry of activity building smaller strong points all along the coast defending possible landing sites.

Typically, in Normandy, a German strong point or 'Widerstandsnest' would have one to three field guns, two or three anti-tank guns (50mm, one 88mm if possible), mortars; up to thirty machine-guns and would also be ringed with barbed wire. Some were behind anti-tank ditches and/or minefields. Only the machine-guns and rifles (short range weapons) fired straight at the beach. A strong point's larger guns were sited to fire toward the shore line at an angle, raking long stretches of beach and engaging enemy forces attacking other strong points to the right and left. Angling orientation also made the main bunkers and casemates harder to spot from the sea or beach and permitted strong concrete walls and mounded earth facing the sea and warship guns.

Less powerful positions also proliferated, filling in the spaces between major strong points and at less likely invasion sites. These German photos were designed to show universal readiness and capability. They ignore the innervating duty of months standing watch with little cover and no threat at hand. Nor do they deal with thousands of troops removed from combat, their support requirements and the cost of maintaining their stations.

Above is a primitive, cold and windy, anti-aircraft position. About all a German soldier could say about this duty was 'beats being on the Eastern Front'.

Below, a permanent installation with plenty of concrete and three armored open-back turrets for the guns (possibly 4.7″ French). The background bunker is for observation, ranging and control.

Gun positions similar to those on the previous page but without the concrete scarp. Barbed wire and rising land show this position is inland from the coast.

Below, armored protection and camouflage netting for the heavy guns but the troops are living in tents. This may be the same gun shown on page 13.

This photograph shows a heavy coastal battery. Note the ventilators for the personnel who operation from below.

Propaganda photos of seemingly impregnable gun positions were intended to intimidate, or influence the inevitable invasion to go elsewhere.

In early 1944 Field Marshal Rommel had enough experience with Allied control of the air to understand he would have trouble moving powerful maneuver units to an invasion sector. An invasion would have to be defeated on the beach.

A flurry of activity followed. Some defenses were cheap and easily installed. Of course there was the expected thousands of miles of barbed wire entanglements. Hundreds of thousands of anti-personnel and anti-tank mines were planted on the most likely beaches.

A lot of information filtered out of occupied Europe, even including photographs. At left is part of a British report on Atlantic Wall defenses.

The Soviets were increasing pressure on the Allies for an Invasion in the west to pull German troops from the Eastern Front. That meant the return to Western Europe would have to come sometime in early 1944. The Germans knew that too and accelerated construction of beach defenses.

This shows a common type of coastal battery which will still be seen.

Yet another type of layout for coastal batteries.

16

This casemate near Le Havre was completed but not yet earthed when it was overrun by Allied troops four months after the invasion. It was part of a four gun 155mm battery located 17 miles northeast of the Normandy landing beaches and a potential threat to invasion shipping straying too far east. Twenty-four such batteries (of various hardness and gun-size) were built, or building, in Normandy between Le Havre and Cherbourg. In June 1944, some guns had been withdrawn inland while their earthen emplacements were converted to concrete. Those weapons didn't threaten the invasion.

Everything at hand was used to create invasion barriers, the cheaper the better because quantity was important. **Below**, a Belgian beach with concrete bunkers in the background and an old Renault tank turret (shown with the gun removed) as a strong point.

Some remote beaches were only sparsely defended by the most primitive systems – in this case at Gironde, France, a light artillery piece, barbed-wire entanglement and a few posts beyond the high-water mark. Those dunes were also probably mined.

The Germans also produced wire-guided mini-tanks packed with explosives to take out attackers (several of these were found on Utah Beach but artillery fire cut their control wires and they didn't operate right so did no damage).

← Der „Grabenwolf". Ferngelenkt, wird dieser Liliputpanzer, der eine Sprengladung schleppt, für Spezialaufgaben verwendet

Allied invasion planners faced the challenge of where, when and how, and how to get information while maintaining some element of surprise.

Task One would be to select beaches that could take the large forces to be involved.

Task Two was to devise ways to get onto the beaches without prohibitive losses.

Task Three would be get forces through the Atlantic Wall, off the beach and pushing inland behind the defenses.

For answers, Allied planners turned to aerial photoreconnaissance.

Chapter II

AERIAL
PHOTORECONNAISSANCE

Long before Operation Overlord was in planning, the RAF was routinely taking aerial photos of German-held Europe as part of normal intelligence collection to see what the enemy was up to. **Below** is Ouistreham, eastern end of the future Sword Beach, on 31 July 1942. We see the Caen Canal and locks and Orne River curving to the sea farther east. Lines drawn on the print indicate aircraft nadir – important for mapping.

There hasn't been much bombing damage and there weren't many defenses yet – most German military resources were going elsewhere at this point and the concept of stopping an invasion on the beaches was two years in the future.

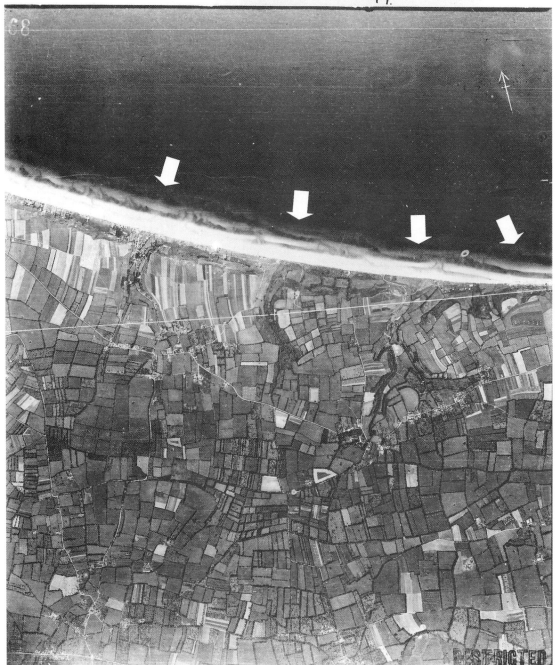

Above is the future Omaha Beach on 18 August 1942, from the left my arrows show: Les Moulins Draw; Saint-Laurent/La Sapiniere Draw; Le Cavey/Colleville Draw; and La Revolution on the far right. Vierville Draw is off the left side of the frame. The scale of this imagery made it useful for mapping and as a 'base line' to gauge future activity, but was so small-scale it provided little Intelligence value on defenses.

Tide is partly out and the beach looks deceptively clear and inviting for invasion.

Below, mouth of the Orne and Caen Canal, 27 August 1942. A small defense position (probably anti-aircraft) seems to be installed at the upper arrow. It doesn't appear that work has begun on the Merville Battery (lower arrow). Horsa Bridge is at lower left.

RLLS: F2A: 140: 27·8·42: 12": SHEET 40/16 N.W.

Once the landing area was tentatively identified, photo recce began to collect more frequently and more systematically. Missions had to be run carefully because undue emphasis on a given shore might give the enemy ideas and eliminate surprise. Starting in late 1943, the number of recce flights over Occupied France from increased dramatically. Some of this effort was hidden inside the intense and obvious recon hunt for German flying bomb launch sites.

Below is Les Moulins Draw; Omaha Beaches 'Dog Red' and 'Easy Green', at high tide on 14 January 1944. Note unoccupied artillery positions and personnel trenches atop the bluffs. Since the draw would naturally channel attackers, defenses were arranged accordingly. Strong concrete gun and machine-gun emplacements were built on either side of the draw mouth.

Shadows show a relatively low ridge/sea wall just beyond the high-water mark and gradually rising land inland to a substantial cliff (100–170') blocking access to the flat, open fields beyond. A few natural breaks in the cliffs are shown by roads going inland from the beach. Those draws would have to be used to get vehicles up onto the flat, open ground where maneuver was possible. It was expected that each draw would be defended from the heights as well as below in the swale and buildings just beyond the beach.

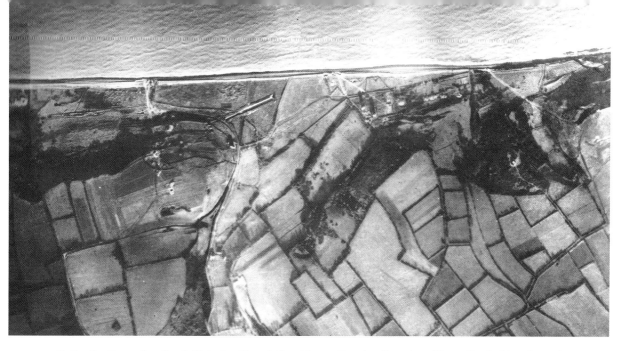

Colleville Draw (on the left) to La Revolution Draw, Omaha Beaches 'Easy Red', 'Fox Green' and 'Fox Red' as they were on 14 January 1944. Paths up from the beaches skirt cliffs and easily defended high ground, making them a 'shooting gallery'. Note how the Colleville Draw route is steep enough to force circling east to make the climb inland.

A tank trap (ditch wider than an armored vehicle tracks can span with sides too steep for the tank to climb) has been begun to further deny access to a negotiable slope leading to open ground inland and force vehicles into a 'killing zone' ranged by anti-tank weapons. Enlargement disclosed no other significant defenses under construction.

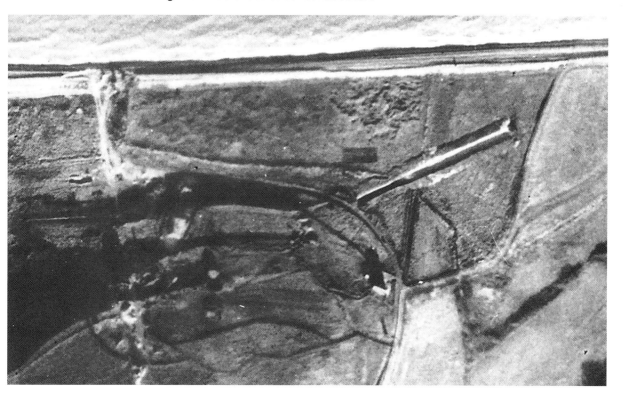

Ponte du Hoc showed considerable activity on 15 February 1944, the sort of photo interpreters like to analyze. A lot of dirt has been moved and five gray circles in a 'V' generally facing north suggest positions being created for large guns. Located ten miles east of Utah Beach and four miles west of Omaha Beach, long-range guns here would pose a significant threat to naval and troop ships supporting the beaches, to say nothing of potential fire on the beaches themselves. Even without guns, German observation from here would be a threat to the invasion.

At high tide there is almost no beach at this location.

Enlargement of the Ponte du hoc imagery provides a better look at early construction of at least five sites that could develop into bunkers. This could reasonably be assumed to be part of the chain of positions for large artillery that were strung about every 20 miles along the coast, but no details can yet be discerned. Measurement of the assumed gun positions ruled out the super heavy weapons, but they had sufficient diameter to house up to 155mm field artillery pieces. Lack of rail access to the site also ruled out larger weapons.

Vertical imagery was supplemented by obliques that showed the same areas from a different perspective. This is Houlgate, a typical Normandy seaside town eight miles east of the future Sword Beach, on 24 February 1944.

Many beach defenses at this time were still simply close-set posts that would be just under water at high tide to block or overturn landing craft.

0058   R173 414 24 FEB 44//W20"

Pointe du Hoc again, this time in a lower tide on 8 March 1944, showing the width of beach shingle below the 100 foot cliffs. Shadow shows formidable cliffs to east and west of the point with no beach to speak of and no nearby draws providing ready access to higher ground from the beach.

Note the five revetments at the far right – possible positions for light field artillery. One even appears occupied (the upper right). Breaking the existing farm field patterns indicates a military purpose. However, the lack of track activity leading to them is suspicious. Guns had to be towed into position by something, and that should leave tracks.

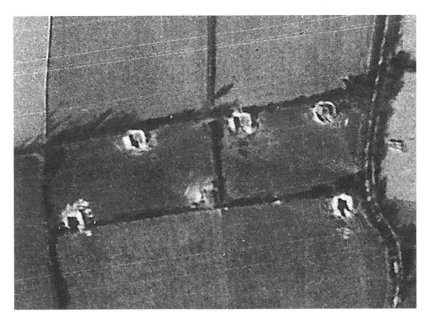

Enlargement of the 8 March Pointe du Hoc imagery shows there are now six probable gun emplacements, three nearing completion, none occupied. Well-developed trenches defend the site.

In three months this draw would be heavily defended – and Omaha Beach landing sites 'Dog White', 'Dog Red', and 'Easy Green'.

Shadows show the nearly vertical cliffs at Les Moulins Draw, 8 March 1944. It's low tide but reflected light has washed out most of the beach coverage. The draw now has trenches and firing positions on heights overlooking the town and anti-tank ditches to stop or canalize vehicles trying to get off the beach. Intelligence could reasonably assume that at least some of the buildings near the entrance of the draw have been converted to firing positions for machine guns and anti-tank weapons. Confirmation of that information would come from French sources on the ground.

Omaha Beach Saint-Laurent Draw (La Spiniere) on 8 March. It is tempting to call the four apparent revetments on high ground to the left possible artillery positions, but again the lack of tracks is troubling, so is the narrow access in each revetment (guns have to enter somehow). There are, however, new trench/firing positions immediately above the beach directly in line with the small road leading inland. A straight road up from the swale indicates a more gradual slope than some of the other draws, and the mouth of this one is also wider. There is considerable trench activity on flat land just above the high-water line.

Le Cavey/Colleville Draw to La Revolution (Omaha 'Easy Red' to 'Fox Green') on 8 March 1944. The largest initial landings, and heaviest casualties, would occur here.

The tank-trap blocking access inland has been extended since January and track activity indicates active improvement of defenses on the heights above the curving road.

Sword Beach ('Queen White', 'Queen Red', 'Roger Green'), the left flank of the invasion, on 28 May 1944. Note bomb craters at lower right – clearly misses of some target nearer the coast.

Note the complete lack of trenches, anti-tank ditches, strong points or encampments in the countryside behind the coast.

Future 'Queen Red' beach. Enlargement shows German strong point (Widerstandsnest) WN 20 and the beach in front of it with two definite lines of off-shore obstacles about 100 yards out. This was the most formidable position on Sword Beach with eight 50mm anti-tank guns, four 75mm howitzers and one of the much feared 88mm anti-tank weapons. Trenches linking large beach houses show where they have been converted to defense positions for machine-guns and riflemen.

Only one other area on the 28 May photo was suspicious, showing moved earth near the beach and back up a wooded hill behind the coast road. Trenches were a definite sign of defensive improvements. This would be 'Roger Green' beach on 6 June.

Ouistreham on 28 May 1944. Sword landings 'Roger White' and 'Roger Red' (closest to the Orne mouth), would be here on D-Day. A new anti-tank ditch carved through the city was as destructive as a stick of bombs dropped earlier.

Below, enlargement shows development of bunkers and trenches for a strong point. This would be the east end of British 3rd Division landings. It is hard to identify bunkers and casemates because earth disturbed by bombing looks the same as new construction.

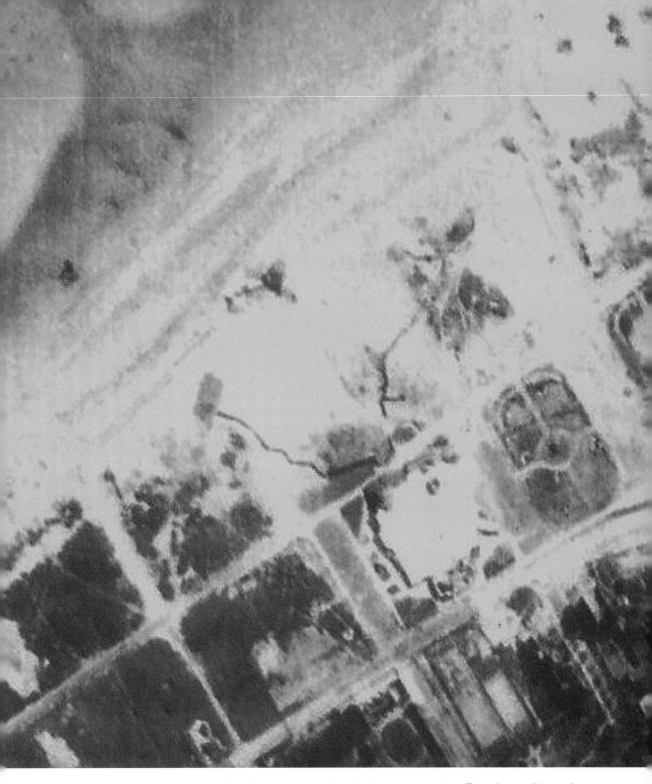

About 1,500 feet west of the Orne was another obvious strong point. Trenches call attention to the area and structures not aligned with the road system are immediately suspicious as gun positions. Future 'Roger White' landings would be here.

34 R368 268 18MAR44//X14"

It was important to get a good look at beach defenses from all angles and all tidal situations. This 18 March 1944 RAF coverage was probably made with a forward oblique camera. I found it in retired files of the Office of Naval Intelligence.

These seven successive lines of vertical posts are unsophisticated: simple materials, easy and quick to install with local labor. The 6 June landings faced obstacles much more complex and effective.

A frame from a 14 April 1944 RAF run along the coast using an oblique camera. The tide is out to best show the extent of off-shore beach defenses.

039

R466 2 14APR44 ||22C20 71I/7

More of the 14 April run. Photoreconnaissance aircraft had to make dangerous 'dicing'[3] missions like this from Pas-de-Calais to Cherbourg lest the real focus of collection activity in Normandy tip off the Germans as to the intended landing areas.

Dicing let planners see how beach obstacles were constructed and anchored; get a better look at bunkers, casemates and machine-gun nests facing the beaches; and see the beach exits from a different aspect.

In this case beach obstacles are a mix of wooden posts and concrete-frame pyramids (see next Chapter).

---

3. A term dating from WWI when low altitude flights over enemy territory were referred to as 'dicing with the Devil'.

The low-flying 'photo bird' scared workmen using a pile driver to set posts in the beach. Behind the lines of vertical posts are the more effective 'Czech Hedgehogs'.

At least eight men are shown. Two lie on the sand at right, two are running left. The rest are 'bailing out' from some sort of framework in the center.

Someone in HQ must have looked at the dicing imagery and said, 'Great stuff. The lower the better'. On 19 May 1944 US 10th Photo Group (10PG) pilots took up the challenge and returned a series of dangerous ultra-low flights.

0093 (US 30/4000)19 MAY 44(F/12)//IOPG

This USAAF 30 Squadron (10 Photo Group) F-5 flew low over the beaches at low tide with a 12″ focal-length Forward Oblique camera.

This is another example showing that there was no 'standard' beach. The same off-shore obstacles were used, but arrangements varied considerably. In this case a line of ramp obstacles form the outer-most defense, some appear to be topped with mines. Next came a line of posts, some also topped with mines. Those defenses fronted densely scattered, and more effective, pyramids and 'Czech Hedgehogs'.

In full tide, all these would be under water.

Slender posts in the foreground are curious. They appear to be for a light fence. My guess would be a line warning workers not to pass along the beach—perhaps because of mines buried in the sand.

41

Vierville, 19 May 1944. The nacelle tells us this is the right oblique camera (RO) of an F-5 (photo version of the P-38) heading east. Any lower and props would be kicking up water. Speed was too high and altitude too low for the IMC (image motion compensation) in vertical cameras to compensate and images would be blurred, so only right and left high oblique cameras could be used. As it is, objects close to the aircraft are out of focus. 10PG flew eleven of these low-altitude beach recon missions in May, losing two pilots.

Below, tide is out and enlargement shows the most deadly and effective beach obstacle, 'Belgian Gates'. Randomly positioned well out from the shore and placed to be under water at high tide, the 'Gates' were sturdy and well anchored, making them capable of stopping, capsizing or ripping the bottom out of a landing craft.

'Czech Hedgehogs' and ramps at Les Moulins (Omaha Draw D3), 19 May 1944. Note the off-shore defenses are situated well beyond the high-water mark. Dark or boarded up windows indicate most buildings were unoccupied—or being converted to firing positions.

This dicing coverage went on for 250 exposures on the RO and LO cameras. Six inch lenses were used. The sortie was far too low to use the vertical camera of the Tri-Metragon installation.

It is interesting to note the off-shore defenses at many other beaches are more primitive in construction and less dense than those at the Omaha beaches. Apparently the Germans identified Omaha as a likely landing site just as did the Allied planners in England so Omaha got the 'full treatment'.

Enlargement of Les Moulins oblique coverage shows German activity indicated by freshly turned earth near the water. We can't see the anti-tank ditch from this angle, nor can we see German strong points atop the bluffs on either side of the draw (apparently built between March and June).

Numbers above equate to things on the 8 March vertical photo below.
Identifying matching buildings or objects allowed views to be compared from different angles and helped planners understand what they were facing.

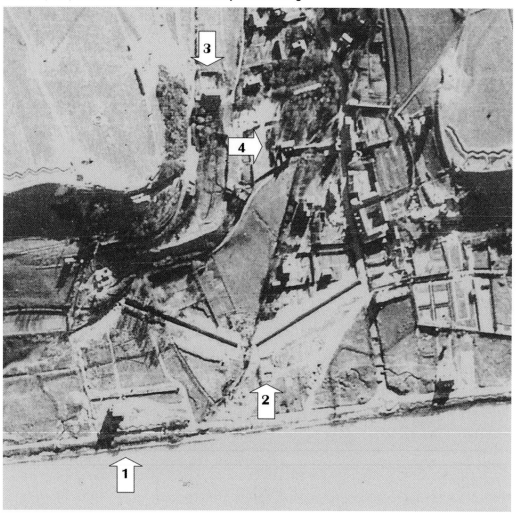

Above, work parties on the sands at low tide, Saint-Laurent, Omaha Draw E1, 19 May 1944. Ramps, a 'gate' variation and hedgehogs.

Below, enlargement shows the building unoccupied (you can see right through the upper floor). The ramp running up the hill may be a skid-way to get gravel to the site of casemates under construction on the heights.

When I finished with the RO (right oblique) and began to roll the LO on my light table I was astounded to see that, for at least part of the 19 May mission, the pilot had been flying inside the outer perimeter of beach defenses, making this (as far as I've seen) one of the outstanding, and most daring, 'dicing' sorties of the war. The aircraft shadow says it all.

I also discovered a surprise at the start of one of the rolls of film. On his way to France, the pilot spotted something small and curious on the otherwise open sea far below him. As good recce pilots will do, he flipped on a camera to catch it. Had he been shot down, and his film recovered, I wonder what the Germans would have concluded from an extreme enlargement showing one of the Phoenix artificial harbor segments under tow somewhere off southern England.

Allied Intelligence knew a lot about conditions in France from agents and high and low altitude aerial photoreconnaissance. **Above** is an undated, low-altitude oblique of 82nd Airborne objective; Sainte-Mere-Eglise. The well-known church and courtyard are upper left.

Left, Carentan from the same photo series, looking northeast.

Right, Cherbourg, from the same series but possibly taken before the war from higher ground or a taller building. Allied Intel was interested in the port in the background.

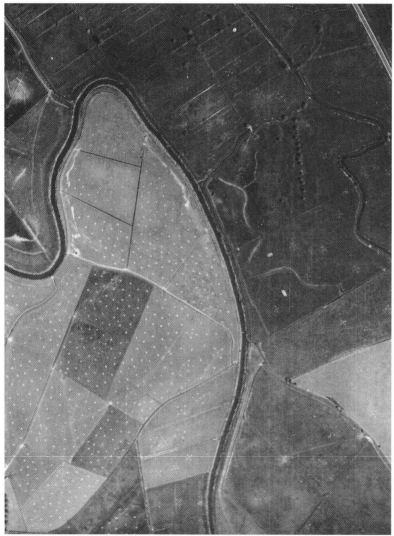

Every possible airborne landing site was covered by recon in the search for safe fields near tactical objectives. This is a broad, flat, dry area on the Vire River, near the Caen-Cherbourg rail line (seen at upper right). This is three miles south of Isigny sur Mer on 28 May 1944.

Those white dots show spoil from vertical posts, 'Rommel Asparagus', set out in rows to interrupt a glider landing.

German engineers apparently deemed the east side of the Vire too marshy for a glider landing.

OSS Agents photographed a typical 'Asparagus' field near Cherbourg after Allied troops controlled the land. Cheap and easily installed by local labor without elaborate equipment, some of the posts were topped with Teller Mines and trip-wires.

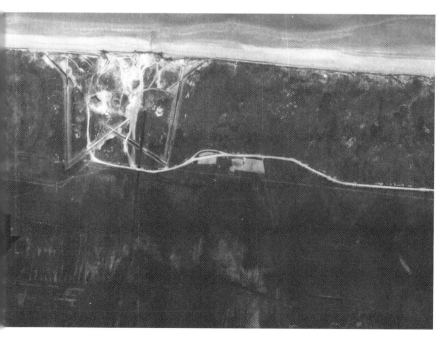

Taking a significant risk, the Allies laid on high altitude photo recon of Invasion Beaches on 4 June 1944, just one day before the scheduled invasion. This enlargement is the ditch-defended strong point at planned Utah Beach 'Tare Green'.

Farther east, named the 'Redoubt', this strong point defended beach 'Uncle Red', the center of planned Utah landings. Note trenches and firing positions immediately above the beach. Easily seen inland are swampy fields that wouldn't support heavy vehicles. That made trafficable avenues away from the beaches all the more critical in Allied planning, thus the 82nd and 101st Airborne Division landings further inland to gain control of the few viable routes between the beaches and solid ground.

More 4 June 1944 Utah coverage, farther east. Currents swept many landing craft here and this became Utah Beach on 6 June. Enlargement shows extensive light defensive works (for riflemen and machine guns) but an easy gradient off the beach – and a serious lack of multiple routes inland. Success at Utah depended upon quickly securing that road.

Chapter III

UNDERSTANDING THE DEFENSES

Marshal Rommel knew he had insufficient troop strength and quality, particularly in powerful maneuver units like Panzers that had made the Wehrmacht so effective in earlier years. He was well aware that the Atlantic Wall was paper thin, and given Allied control of the local air, moving reinforcements to a breach would result in many losses before combat began. He concluded that an invasion would have to be stopped on the beaches.

Beaches in Normandy had high tides (17 to 21 feet) and long gradients (as much as 500 yards difference between high and low water marks at Omaha). The Field Marshal believed the Allies would land at high water to minimize exposure to small arms fire from German troops in positions directly defending the beaches.

Based upon that assumption he created a 'Devil's Garden' of passive defenses that would be under water, invisible and unavoidable, at high tide. These defenses would snag landing craft, rip out their bottoms, blow them up, cause them to swamp or swing sideways to fire from the shore, and snarl the way for subsequent vessels. They would also force heavy-laden troops into water from waist deep to over their heads.

Allied troops expected to encounter bunkers, occupied trenches, tank traps, artillery, machine-gun positions, even armor. Some of them had faced all that before in North Africa and Italy, many hadn't. The off-shore beach obstacles were something new. They ranged from simple posts to concrete or steel shapes. All were intended to make it as difficult as possible for troops to struggle to the beach against mortar, machine-gun and anti-tank gun fire. Mines were frequently added to obstacles to multiply the damage.

The more elaborate off-shore obstacles featuring steel and welding, poured concrete and complex installation, were the earliest efforts, occurring in the most obvious landing sites. Urgency caused by the clearly impending invasion resulted in an increased use of wooden posts. Those were sunk on beaches and just inland by the hundreds of thousands.

Most of the following photos of beach obstacle types were taken near Cherbourg by OSS teams after the city fell to the Allies, but all the shapes were known and understood by Allied planners because of photo recon before the invasion.

The most elaborate beach defense in wide use was the 'Belgian Gate'. Well braced, welded steel, these were solid enough to stop even a large landing craft ramming into them. In lower tides, landing craft would be slowed, making better targets as they tried to thread a path through the gates. With high tides, the 'gates' would be under water. Landing craft would be caught, hull possibly holed, in water too deep for troops to disembark.

'Belgian Gates' were most effective when used in large numbers, forming a zone with considerable depth, leaving no clear avenues to the beach. Note a wide area of open beach beyond the 'gates'. They were of less value when uncovered by a receding tide – except that they tended to force landing craft to stop well short of dry land.

'Gates' were well anchored, but, on D-Day, experience showed a heavily loaded, large landing craft with good speed might ram through one. The only way to get rid of the 'Gates' was for Engineers to blow them up.

This appears to be a photo of pre-fabricated 'Belgian Gates' faces awaiting installation. The gravel access road hints at many more of them here at one time. They are stored between steel rail posts and a barbed-wire field designed to frustrate an airborne landing.

This type of elaborate and expensive barrier may have only occurred at one site. Pre-shaped rails in the foreground indicate it was still under construction and it appears to be a very labor-intensive job. Perhaps the plan was to eventually move them off-shore. Location above the high-water line is hard to explain (perhaps as a tank barrier?).

More common concrete pyramids are along the same beach scarp in the background. Note, the tide is in and there is almost no beach at the bottom of the scarp.

'Pyramids' were pre-formed concrete sections. Six wired together created the shape. These were easy to make and easy to assemble but they were not well anchored, depending upon their weight and shape for resistance. Here they are seen backed by rows of angling posts, some topped with Teller Mines. This whole defense field would slow, but probably couldn't stop, a determined landing.

A closer look at 'Pyramids' shows their construction. Given a few minutes, Engineers could easily blow-up or disassemble this type of defense.

Designed to hole a landing craft, 'Czech Hedgehogs' were particularly effective. Made of steel rails in a shape similar to medieval Caltrops, like the other obstacles they were sited to be just below the surface at high tide to rip the bottom out of landing craft and dump troops into 'killing zones' in deep water. Though not anchored, they always presented several sharp arms if bumped or rolled. These were some of the most prevalent defenses at Omaha Beach. Ironically, some landing troops pinned down short of the beach by heavy fire from the cliffs were able to shelter behind the steel rails of 'Hedgehogs' and survive.

Both photos show how hedgehogs looked in partial flood and how they were placed in rows and close-spaced. Being relatively low they could be a hazzard close in to shore.

The same beach at higher tide shows hedgehogs at water's edge, some of the out-lying obstacles going under water.

Pressure to block more beaches quickly resulted in simply driving wooden posts into the sands. Vertical posts were fast and easy to seat. Angling made them more likely to withstand the shock of a landing craft. Note at least five are topped with mines, seemingly installed at random.

The foreground shows three 'Pyramids' either ready for installation or recently disassembled by Allied Engineers.

Concrete ramps, often topped with mines, were intended to tip a landing craft or turn it broadside. An approaching landing craft would be coming from the right.

This photo shows the three pre-formed concrete shapes and how the ramp was sited just past rows of posts. Landing craft might go over the posts but ramps were often higher. Note some 'Pyramids' in the background.

More primitive wooden ramps were quickly created and could be quite substantial, standing higher – judging from the man, about 9-10 feet high. Perhaps the height indicates an unusually large tidal rise at this site. This ramp is topped by a mine. Enough of these crude devices and approaching a beach would be quite hazardous.

This beach hadn't received the complete treatment yet. The posts are too few and too far apart to be much of an impediment. Almost submerged in the water are prefabricated 'Pyramids' of a different design. A partly disassembled/destroyed 'Pyramid' is at the far right.

Some beach defenses were either really basic, or perhaps done by local workers who didn't understand the requirements. The posts are hefty enough but sparsely placed couldn't have much effect. I can't tell if those are explosive charges or simply 'spacers' between the posts.

Some beaches had mines above the high-water mark, perhaps even a little way off-shore. Mines buried in deeper water would be made useless by a few tidal changes. Beaches seeded with mines would be neutralized by 'flail tanks' using rotating drums with heavy chains to beat the surface and, hopefully, detonate mines harmlessly ahead of the vehicle. Other vehicles designed to solve specific problems getting beyond the beaches were: tanks with heavy mortars or flame-throwers to take out bunkers; tanks with fascines to fill in anti-tank ditches or unroll matting to give tanks and trucks purchase on loose beach shingle; tanks with 'dozer' blades or small assault bridges; and tanks that could 'wade' in deep water or 'swim' ashore (Duplex Drive M4 'Sherman' tanks). Collectively they were called 'Hobart's Funnies' after their commander, Maj. Gen. Percy Hobart.

This Matilda Flail was photographed in North Africa where the technique was first successfully employed.

Invasion planners had the daunting task of balancing a bewildering series of variables against the probabilities of success and the lives of men. Landing at low tide would expose all the beach obstacles for avoidance, but would force the men to transit up to 500 yards of open ground under fire just to reach the shore berms. High tide landings would result in losses from running into the obstacles. Then there was the requirement for a surprise night attack with enough moonlight to permit precise parachute and glider landings. It was finally decided that the best combination of tides and moon was met on 5 June 1944.

Operation Overlord beach landings would be made just after dawn, about an hour after low tide. Many beach obstacles would be visible and rising tide would float off hard-beached landing craft to clear the beach and make other trips possible. Once on the land, forces would rapidly thrust inland to create a defense perimeter while sappers and engineers would begin destroying the off-shore obstacles, creating safe lanes to the beaches for subsequent landings by larger vessels bringing more men, heavy vehicles and equipment. By the next low tide (1725 hrs.), Bulldozers and explosive charges were expected to have made short work of beach defenses below the high-tide mark.

Chapter IV

THE FIRST IN

Nothing on the scale of D-Day had ever been attempted. The scope was as staggering as the obstacles to be overcome ashore. Planners knew it would be touch-and-go until sufficient force could be built-up and lodgments deepened to effective defensive perimeters against the expected counterattacks. The Allies pulled out all the stops with deception, swimming tanks, artificial harbors and a fuel pipeline under the English Channel. There would be fire from ships off the invasion beaches and bombing by heavy, medium, light and fighter bombers to isolate the invasion area and reduce the possibility of enemy reinforcements. Disrupting enemy communications and troop movements behind the invasion beaches was a high priority and weeks before D-Day Allied aircraft began interdicting lines-of-communication as far north and east as Paris. There was no doubt about elite American and British parachute and airlanding infantry units being in the mix. They became Operation Neptune.

No one was under any illusions that surprise would make Neptune landings unopposed, and the 82nd Airborne's 505th Parachute Infantry Regiment (PIR) was the only unit jumping that had prior experience in combat (Operation Husky, Sicily, July 1943).

Units stepped up training in England. **Right**, gliders practice flight and landing in April 1944.

Shadows are well out in front of the aircraft but the spread is less on the lead ships. The C-47 at upper right is atop the shadow of the Waco CG-4 it is towing, showing this flight is descending.

Everyone understood that PIRs would go in first and drops had to be tight for the best chance of success, but none of the Troop Carrier pilots in Overlord had experience flying into anti-aircraft fire. It was also understood that if the invasion faltered on the beaches all the paratroopers would probably be lost.

The scope of Neptune is evident in this photo of a single UK base training glider pilots in May 1944. I count 19 C-47 tow planes, 24 Horsa gliders in two-tone British camouflage livery, 78 Waco gliders with U.S. markings and olive drab paint, one B-24, one U/I light plane and one possible B-25. And this is only part of one base. For some reason the string of Waco gliders and C-47 tugs lined up for take-off on the runway is short one glider.

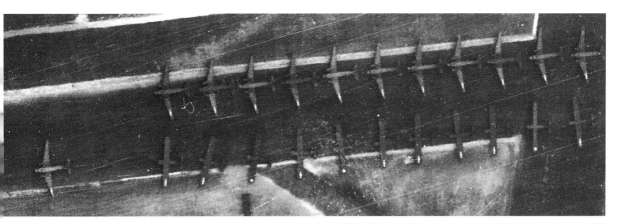

Enlargements of the same imagery (**above and right**) show the relative size and shape of a C-47, a Horsa and two Wacos. Black and White invasion identification stripes weren't painted yet.

As we've seen, the Germans were also preparing for the obvious, concentrating defenses on the beaches but not neglecting likely glider landing grounds.

Much like the British had done in Kent in 1940, obstructions were created in large open fields. Obstruction posts were small hindrance to paratroops but they were a real hazard for gliders, designed to tear off wings or flip them onto their backs. However, surprise and swift use of a concentrated force were so important that landing near the ground objectives was critical. So many of the most desirable landing grounds were studded with 'Rommelspargel' that in the end defenses were largely disregarded in favor of proximity to the target.

Parachute Infantry and air landing units were to spread confusion in the enemy rear, secure critical bridges and roads, sever enemy communications to the interior and, for a brief period, keep enemy reinforcements at bay. Since they needed surprise, night drops and glider landings were unavoidable. High casualties and confusion were anticipated, but the risk was deemed acceptable when weighed against the potential gain.

British beaches were the east flank of the invasion and their left was supported by British 6th Airborne Division (mostly landing east of the Orne River). Parachute and airlanded troops had the tasks of destroying a strong German coastal artillery position near the coast two miles east of the landing beaches. They would also control key bridges over the Caen Canal and Orne River to block enemy reinforcements. They had to hold their ground until relieved by advancing forces from the beachhead. Surprise was considered so important in taking of the two bridges that those assault units were the first to land in France on D-Day.

Photo Reconnaissance aircraft were lifting off for France before first light on 6 June.

Extensive cloud cover would ordinarily scrub a photo mission, but not this day. It was critical to determine what was going on in France.

Heavy cloud cover in some areas and scattered clouds in others were problems most of the morning. Recon imagery also picked up photos of D-Day activity. Here eight P-47s trolling for enemy planes or hovering overhead to support ground troops.

Combing the coast, recce planes photographed P-38s orbiting to insure air superiority over the beaches.

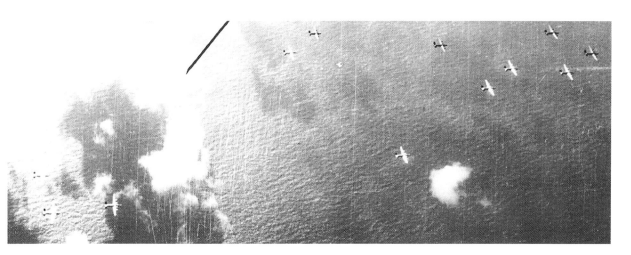

Flights of heavy bombers, in this case USAAF B-24s, were photographed shuttling from England to bomb targets behind the FEBA (Forward Edge of the Battle Area).

Flying high or low, alone or in pairs, recce sorties sometimes caught a wingman (a USAAF F-5).

Imagery available to me during my file screening was selected cut-negatives from RAF missions and roll negatives from USAAF sorties. Some missions I reviewed combed parallel to the coast at different distances, others (as we shall see later) flew perpendicular to the coast, going inland for several miles, then turning and exiting on a reciprocal heading several miles east or west. None of the film was accompanied by plots but I had good maps and I found Google satellite photos invaluable – sorry, I wasn't able to identify every location that caught my eye three decades ago.

Photo reconnaissance missions on 6 June 1944 also captured assembling support ships and the characteristic 'fish tailing' wakes of a line of flat-bow LCAs or Higgins Boats heading for the beach.

Flying just off shore, directly over the beach or paralleling the coast at various distances inland from the beach, dozens of sorties collected hundreds of 250 and 500 foot-long rolls of negatives (sometimes five rolls per flight) that were rushed back to England for processing and photo interpretation.

In spite of high winds that scattered some of their parachute drops, the 6th Airborne Division made a 'text book' airborne assault with gliders coming down almost on top of the two target bridges. Troops assembled swiftly and controlled both bridges in ten minutes – accomplishing all four assigned tasks by dawn.[4] The rest of the division jumped in about two hours later.

This photo shows a 'Horsa', and the wing of another, on the ground just a few feet from the bascule bridge spanning the Caen Canal west of Benouville. The bridge counter-weight section is visible in the image, as are German trenches on the west side of the canal.

RAF and USAAF photoreconnaissance aircraft were out early and often on the 6th, this time not so much searching for the enemy activity as to help discover where forces, particularly airborne, actually landed, and what progress was being made.

The main photo recce task was providing confirmation of invasion progress to Allied commanders 'sweating it out' in England.

Keeping all those flights sorted out was quite a tour-de-force, made more complex by heavy, medium and fighter bombers also working the same airspace. I've never heard of a mid-air in all that activity but there were a few collisions between gliders and aircraft over the channel on the way in or back to England.

---

4. Honoring this coup, the Orne River Ranville Bridge is now names for British Horsa gliders and the critical Caen Canal Benouville Bridge for Pegasus, the 6th Airborne Division unit emblem.

When a flood of men began to arrive from the air, the Germans were just as unable to sort out and stop what was going on as were the Dutch and Belgians in 1940. Following sharp fighting, the Merville Battery was neutralized by dawn. It was discovered to have four obsolete 100mm guns instead of the expected more threatening modern 150mm guns. Linked up with infantry advancing from Sword Beach, British Airborne Infantry held the ground east of the Orne for several more days in the face of determined German counterattacks.

Seventeen gliders can be seen on this RAF exposure near the quarry (bottom center) between Amfreville and Ranville (Landing Zone 'N'). The Orne River is down and to the left with the Caen Canal beyond. North, and the coast, are to the top of the photo.

This is where the Normandy Invasion began, just past midnight on 5/6 June.

Enlargement of the photo above is fascinating to a PI. Note the regularly spaced white dots running in a straight line to the upper left corner. That is a newly installed phone line. The route disregarding boundaries of farm fields says it's military – perhaps related to the Merville Battery. Other nearby smaller dots in the fields (slightly closer together) show posts of 'Rommelspargeset' out to disrupt glider landings.

Leading up to the invasion, tactical PR from England was concentrating on the search for V-1 launch sites in France and bombers were attacking those targets as fast as they were identified. On 6th and 7th June all available RAF and USAAF photoreconnaissance and strike assets were assigned tasks directly supporting the invasion.

Invasion beaches were covered every few minutes by PR flights, but coverage of airborne landing zones behind the beaches was not so plentiful. This may be because of morning cloud cover inland, but also because the air behind the beaches was filled with protecting fighters and supporting bombers. Recce sorties were carefully planned to cover programmed Airborne landing zones – and some of the air drops were not where intended.

Another photo of 6th Airborne landing area LZ-N (**below**), looking southwest, shows a piece of the Orne River and Caen Canal just beyond. A little bit of Benouville shows in the upper right corner (on the far side of the canal). The bridge objectives are directly under the cloud (a frustrating but not uncommon circumstance for photo recon). The dark curving shape at upper left is the port propeller of the taking aircraft, an American F-5. Clustered chutes can be seen just right of the propeller tip and 40 gliders are on the ground – one of them between the river and canal very close to the bridges (upper right). Other gliders came down in fields just beyond the upper right corner of this frame.

This photo must have been taken quite early on 6 June because I have seen a photo on the internet (Wikimedia.org) showing the same area with more than a dozen gliders in the same fields where those chutes are on the ground and another (Britannica.com) with at least 80 gliders in the area. All gliders, original assault and reinforcement, appear to have landed heading north, toward the coast (toward the bottom of this photo).

For orientation with modern maps, that white blob just below the cloud is the quarry north of Ranville.

Enlargement shows eighteen Horsas and two Hamilcars (straight wings) down less than a mile from the objective. This was a damn good landing.

Another enlargement of the same imagery, **below**, shows two examples of 'Rommelspargel' clipping the wings of gliders just northeast of the Ranville Quarry. Other Horsas seem to have avoided the hazards and all got down without disaster.

The two US Airborne landings were more scattered. Of course finding the landing zones by spotting gliders and chutes on the ground didn't show where the troops were or how they were doing. Vehicles and heavy guns are relatively simple for a PI to identify but Infantry in contact are a lot harder to spot (fires on the ground are often the best clue). Another factor may have been that a plane flying over and parallel to the beach was assumed friendly but a plane flying perpendicular to the beach (i.e., coming from or going deeper inland) was a question mark and troops on the ground weren't taking any chances.

Twenty plane-loads of pathfinders went in first, landing clean and correct to guide the main landings but the more than 800 aircraft of the main lift didn't fare as well.

Darkness, dense clouds, high winds and fire from now alerted ground forces served to confuse and scatter the transport planes. Some pilots bored in on their drop targets. Others jinked, veered away, speeded up (beyond safe jump conditions), or went to higher altitude, resulting in badly spread drops and drops into locations far from the ground objectives. Tragically, some C-47s went long and heavily-loaded paratroops landed in marsh along the Merderet River, well behind Utah Beach. Some drowned before they could shed their chutes and gear.

Left, this 6 June photo shows 21 chutes and four Waco gliders on the ground, one crashed. It is impossible to tell if the chutes are a stick from the same C-47 but the scattered nature of the landings is apparent. Assembly in the dark was made more difficult by a maze of hedgerows that frustrated the American landings near the Douve River more than the British LZs on the Orne.

Enlargement gives a better look at the Wacos and chutes in fields 3000 feet southwest of Sainte-Marie-du-Mont. This is probably part of the 101st Airborne Division assault.

Utah Beach's left flank hinterland was assigned to the 101st Airborne. Though scattered in their drops and taking losses of men and equipment in the swamps, they successfully secured key bridges around Carentan and causeways leading through low land to the beach. Troops from Utah Beach linked up with the paratroops just after noon.

Behind the right flank of Utah Beach the going was tougher for 82nd Airborne. Their mission was to secure avenues from the beaches, roads near Sainte-Mere-Eglise and bridges over the Merderet River (running farther inland and parallel to the ocean) but intense ground fire caused the loss of many transports and a seriously scattered drop, many on the 'wrong side' of the Merderet. Other men drowned in the Merderet flood-plain or were shot in the air as they descended. Assembly into viable fighting units was slow in the darkness. Ironically, the scattered forces also made it impossible for defenders to determine how many paratroops were landed and what their objectives were.

Another example of the spread landings is the 6 June USAAF photo **below**. There are 14 chutes and 22 gliders (four crashed, one on its back in the open – note fuselage shadow on the wing – and the rest are in trees) dispersed over a little more than a mile of French countryside.

Another enlargement from top right of the preceding photo. This shows the 101st landing 8000 feet southwest of Sainte-Marie-du-Mont. It would be a miracle if anyone got out of that glider unhurt.

Two of these four Wacos came down hard.

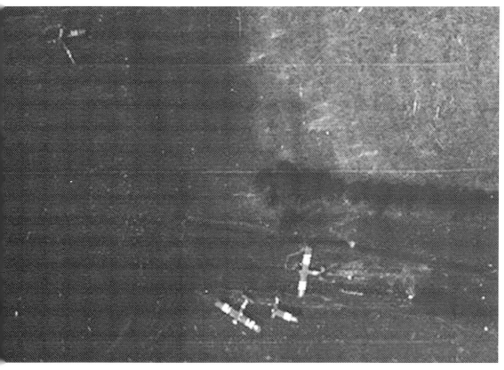

Once a glider committed to land, there was no second chance or 'go around'. **Below**, British Horsas were in a tight landing a little too tight for one pair.

On D-Day, all aircraft, including gliders, wore black and white Invasion Recognition Stripes.

Daylight glider reinforcement on D+1 attempted to bring units back to strength and made the parachute/airlanded infantry viable, vital forces holding the flanks of the invasion. They controlled lines of communication, occupied key intersections and routes, cut telephone wires and disrupted German reinforcements approaching from the south. Aerial photoreconnaissance in clearer weather on 7 June documented airlanding reinforcements and helped locate drop areas from the earlier landings.

Some landings were exceptionally well executed – one this clean suggests a day landing. At **left**, six Wacos and a Horsa came down close together, albeit one wound up in the trees. Skids marks show the direction of landing. A number of chutes were in the fields just beyond the upper right of the photo.

Three cows are sauntering over to investigate the upper right Waco, indicating no personnel remaining in the area.

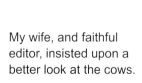

My wife, and faithful editor, insisted upon a better look at the cows.

Enlargement shows a concentrated container air drop by a low-flying bomber, like a B-24, probably for the 82nd Airborne. Some of the chutes are still filling with air so the drop was probably not long before this photo. I don't see any movement nearby but most of the 54 chutes are still attached to their containers, indicating the cargos haven't been unloaded yet. Farm animals (bottom center) suggest no troops or fighting nearby. Parachute containers were used to resupply troops with medicine, ammunition, food, even weapons. The standard was a six foot by 15″ CLE (Central Landing Establishment) container developed by the British. Markings on the outside identified contents to facilitate unloading in combat. The photo (date and location unknown) shows loading a CLE with rounds for the PIAT (Projectile, Infantry, Anti-Tank).

This imagery is a USAAF oblique looking north (to the left as you read this) half way between Sainte-Marie-du-Mont and Sainte-Mere-Eglise on D+1. It is probably a 101st Airborne landing zone. Like many of the others in this book, these fields are still recognizable on Google satellite imagery).

In this example, the choice of LZ (Landing Zone) was excellent – long, flat, dry, and unobstructed by trees, defenses or hedgerows. A good LZ usually contributed a lot to a well-done landing with few casualties. There are more than 50 chutes on the ground, 25 Horsas, six Wacos and one possible Hamilcar. All gliders coming down in or near the same fields suggests a daylight operation and excellent pre-Invasion Intelligence.

Not all landings went as planned and rehearsed. This mosaic of two sequential 6 June photos of an American LZ show gliders coming down in close proximity. It appears the parachutes are from a subsequent supply drop. Pranged Horsas and an intact Waco facing opposite to the Horsas' landing direction, all suggest a night op.

That Horsa facing the Waco has lost part of its left wing to an obstruction of some sort.

A very tight British landing. In spite of a badly broken glider in the hedgerow (left center) and another in the trees (lower right) it looks like everyone got down safe. Marks on the ground indicate approach was from left to right. I have no idea how the glider got into the hedge like that, it might have struck the hedge before it touched down on the ground. Gliders with the tails off have been opened intentionally by their crews to bring out small vehicles such as Jeeps, Universal Carriers or anti-tank guns.

These Horsas probably landed in daylight on 6 June. The jumpers probably came in earlier in the dark.

Another D+1 photo (**above**) shows nearly 100 chutes on the ground, the results of at least four C-47s flying in tight formation, probably indicating the absence of ground fire.

Below is D+1 imagery of British LZ-W on the west side of the Caen Canal (upper left) between Benouville/LePort (arrow) and Saint-Aubin d'Arquenay (just off the bottom of the photo) – Pegasus Bridge is where the road crossing the frame and the canal intersect (just off the left side of the photo). The first of these 46 Horsas came in just after midnight on 6 June. A day later the war had moved south and east. Just off the right edge are bombed German defense positions and tank tracks heading inland (photo in next chapter).

Enlargement of 6th Airborne Division Landing Zone 'W' shows landings to be tight and clean despite occurring at night. It is interesting that, despite being a perfect glider landing area close to obvious military objectives, these broad, open fields beside the Orne, two miles south of Ouistreham, were not filled with obstacles. The only field that is suspicious is the one at bottom center.

Landings were made from south to north (photo bottom). Lord Lovat's Commandos ffollowed the canal bank south from Sword Beach to link with the Airlanding Brigade at Pegasus Bridge just after 1300 hours.

Just before dawn on 6 June, and over the next few days, all three Airborne Divisions were reinforced by additional gliders bringing in light vehicles, more troops, light artillery and anti-tank guns. New landings farther west on D+1 helped isolate the German stronghold port of Cherbourg. A Cellophane-tape repaired 7 June photo (**below**) shows C-47s and Wacos coasting-in just northwest of Utah Beach at low tide. Note off-shore beach defenses at lower left; beached landing craft and Allied support ships at Utah are in the distance.

This is probably the 325th Glider Infantry Regiment being delivered to reinforce 82nd Airborne Division at Sainte-Mere-Eglise.

This series of negatives was RESTRICTED (a security classification we no longer use). The number at lower left was the Intelligence File location for subsequent retrieval.

Below, a companion photo shows a poor choice of landing zone with more than half of the Horsas and Wacos crashed into small fields made by tangles of dense hedgerows and tree lines as more glider tows approach. Despite better options at upper left and right, these Air-Landed troops quickly assembled and bottled up the German garrison in Cherbourg.

It is rare to find imagery of an actual combat air landing in progress.

Use of Horsas for this reinforcement permitted delivery of vehicles and heavier equipment such as howitzers. At **right** we see C-47s with their tows still attached, other gliders on the ground and one at lower right about to touch down. In the center of the photo is a series of white dots that may be a parachute drop (likely supplies).

Another enlargement from the same 7 June photo. Gliders are circling (in a different direction) and it seems a crash at lower left caused a fire.

British landing area near Ranville photographed on D+1. The war has passed on to the south and east, leaving the gliders alone. The Orne River is just beyond the road (below the photo) and the only activity I see is in a field just below the road on the left.

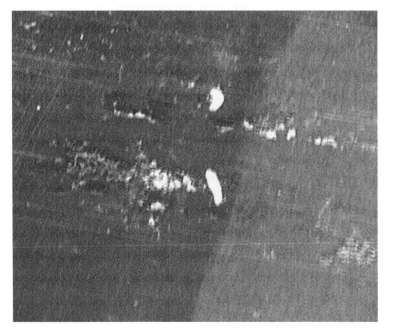

Extreme enlargement shows what appear to be people and scattered material. This is far enough from the nearest glider that it must be related to the chutes and suggests care of injured paratroops.

Chapter V

OVER THE BEACHES

Despite being one of the largest, most complex, best thought-out, best prepared military operations in history, getting onto the Normandy beaches had all the brutal simplicity of a medieval siege. Brave men would hurl themselves in frontal assault at prepared positions manned by equally brave and determined men. The attackers chose the ground; had the advantage of surprise; their forces were concentrated to provide overwhelming numbers at the points of contact. The Allies had complete control of the air and seas and could impede enemy reinforcement behind the beaches. But things were bound to go awry.

Static defenses beyond the high-water mark destroyed a few landing craft, caused others to swamp, even trapped a few to make easy targets for guns on shore, but not enough to frustrate eventual advance onto a given beach.

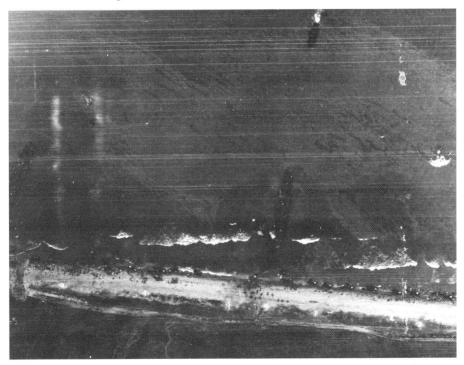

Many landings were just minutes before high tide, counting on what was left of the rising water to float off the initial landing craft. Rising water also meant there was little space for troops between water and sea walls or berms. It they couldn't get off the beaches quickly, they would be trapped on narrow, vulnerable ground.

This photo is early in the invasion (Omaha east of Le Moulins Draw). Troops are bunched up and there is clearly confusion. Only one tank is ashore (forward and left of the beached landing craft). Other landing craft are coming in. A swamped landing craft is off-shore at upper left.

Enlargement gives a better look at the distressed landing craft and seeming chaos on the shore.

Machine-gun and light artillery/anti-tank positions on higher ground took a considerable toll on some beaches but the 'Atlantic Wall' was thin. The key to breaking through that hard crust of defenses was armor. The best progress was on beaches where tanks got ashore early. Anti-tank weapons and mines took out a few tanks, but one-by-one the defensive strong points fell, allowing infantry to spill through into the 'soft' hinterland.

By early afternoon it was clear the invasion was a success. For the rest of 6 June, and the next few days, more men, vehicles, guns and supplies were being landed on the invasion beaches with impunity.

There was little or no prepared German defense behind most beaches so the beachheads expanded rapidly, coalescing and pushing south and west. Behind some beaches, roads heading inland looked like rush hour traffic by mid-afternoon.

Note: each of the five landing areas was divided into specific beaches which were further divided by right (Green) and left (Red). If a center sub-beach was needed it was designated 'White'.

SWORD BEACHES (ROGER, QUEEN, PETER, OBOE)

Britain's 3rd Infantry Division anchored the east end of the invasion, landing on beaches from Ouistreham to Saint-Aubin-sur-Mer. **Below** is 'Queen White' early in the invasion. These men were through the defenses and beyond the beaches in 45 minutes.

Few landing craft have beached yet. Note barrage balloons towed for defense by two of the three Landing Craft Tank vessels (LCTs), deemed necessary, though Allied control of the air was assured by sheer numbers of RAF and USAAF fighters overhead. None of the four long, narrower Landing Craft Infantry (LCIs) had balloons.

Enlargement shows a dozen 'wading' Sherman M4 tanks ashore (arrows show some breathing trunks on the rear deck). I see no Duplex Drive 'swimming' tanks on the beach.

The photo **above** shows mid-morning landings on beaches 'Queen Green' (on left) and 'Queen White'. Many additional LCTs have beached and are unloading. This appears to be an ebbing tide, making it early afternoon. The vessels closest to shore are from the initial landings, firmly grounded until the next rising tide. Those seemingly fixed in position but farther back are a second wave, grounding as the tide goes out. A few of them show propellers churning to push higher to firmly lodge them for safer unloading. At least one LCT has lifted free and is heading back for another load.

At least 150 vehicles of various sizes on the beach and the flow of traffic south prove that German defenses on Sword had collapsed.

Left: British Landing Craft Assault (LCA).

Below, a Landing Craft Tank (LCT) unloading tanks (photo not from D-Day). The British version could carry five tanks. The smaller American LCT carried four.

One reason for success on Sword was the courage of LCT crews risking their vessels against submerged defenses and fire from the shore to ram bows onto the beach and get vital vehicles quickly into action. The two most critical categories were tanks and specialized Engineer vehicles needed to clear on and off-shore obstacles for subsequent landings.

Enlargement of the aerial photo **above** shows (at left) vehicles near the beach. It looks like an Engineer unit heading south – note what appear to be 'dozer' blades or flails sticking out in front of the vehicles. Shadows show them raised to different heights above the road. 'Wader trunks' can be seen on the sterns of most of these tanks. Second from the top and third from the bottom are towing 13.5 foot long 'Porpoise' ammunition and supply sledges.

Enlargement (at **right**) shows a stream of vehicles on the same road south of 'Queen Green', heading toward Caen – 3rd Infantry Division's invasion objective for the first day. The initial easy advance linked up with Airborne forces along the Orne River just after noon. Troops got within three miles of Caen but German resistance stiffened steadily through the afternoon and Caen couldn't be taken in a rush.
Caen was largely destroyed by artillery and aerial bombing before it was finally occupied by the Allies on 18 July.

Note: it is an interesting exercise to match these images with present day Google Satellite photos. The area has seen a lot of development in 67 years, and many of the smaller country towns are almost unrecognizable, but major road alignments, intersections and field patterns don't change. Sometimes you can even identify a large house that still exists as it did in June 1944 (look for characteristic dormers).

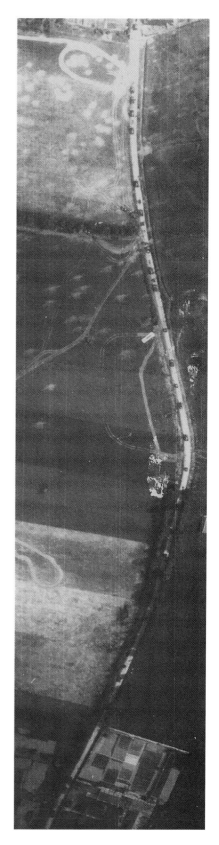

The same road south of the 'Queen Green' beach heading for Hermanville-sur-Mer. Enlargement shows tanks, trucks and Bren Gun Carriers on the road. At least nine armored vehicles are in the field to the left – one clearly a tank. The way the rest are positioned suggests a Self-Propelled Artillery unit deployed to fire southeast.

Those winged splotches scattered through the field (some of us used to call them 'Snow Angels') are classic spoil craters from small caliber high-angle fire such as mortars or light howitzers. Direction of fire is perpendicular to the 'wings' with the source directly opposite to the 'tail' showing on some craters – in this case fire came from the upper left.

'Queen White' beach with eight LCTs and two Landing Craft Infantry (LCIs) aground until the rising tide lifts them off. Those higher on the beach say the tide is going out, probably about noon. Enlargement shows the LCT at far left leaking oil near the bow. It may have been holed by an unseen 'Czech Hedgehog' while grounding with the tide higher.

Above, another enlargement from the preceding vertical showing three beach exits made by Invasion equipment. Engineer vehicles were vital to breaking the beach verge so combat vehicles could exit to dry land and better footing.

Below, (probably D+1 and probably not from Sword), this illustrates why 'Hobart's Funnies' were so important. Wheeled vehicles, even some tracked vehicles, had trouble on the wet sand and unstable shingle. We see a Bulldozer preparing to extricate a truck. 'Czech Hedgehogs' removed from the beach are piled at the right.

'Queen Green' just east of Lion-sur-Mer, fairly early in the invasion. Vehicles are exiting the beach right through a former German strong point.

Enlargement has at least two of 'Hobart's Funnies' (special function tanks – probably Flails) on the beach. These are painted tan instead of Olive Drab like the rest of the equipment. Those vehicles were crucial in removing mines, crossing loose surfaces, spanning ditches and destroying concrete bunkers. At left, four tanks are towing ammunition sledges. The tank with a trailer may be a flame-thrower. Another possible 'Funny' is at far right, perhaps a Dozer tank. Some Engineer M4 guns also took out German bunkers.

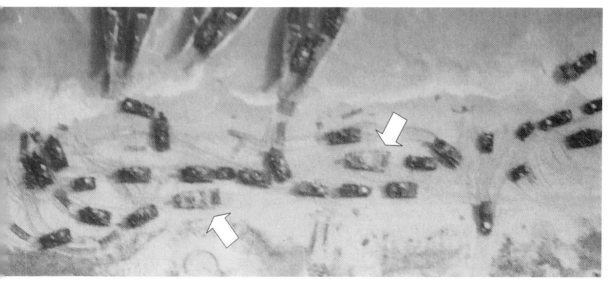

A little farther east, 'Queen Red'. This was marked 1750 hours but that would have been full load tide. It must mean the time the film was processed in England because this is either the ebbing tide or well into the second rising tide – which would peak at 2300 hours. Small movement inland tells me this was taken just after noon. Well-armed bunkers and strong points just beyond this beach resulted in many casualties and held up advance of 2nd Battalion, East Yorkshire Regiment, for about three hours.

Enlargement of German defenses behind 'Queen Red'. Trenches show fighting positions bearing on the beach and its exits. Concrete bunkers are painted camouflage and those on the far right exhibit blast damage.

Below, same imagery, bulldozers have broken paths up off the shingle and 'Bobbin' tanks have laid down matting on both to improve the footing for metal treads of tanks.

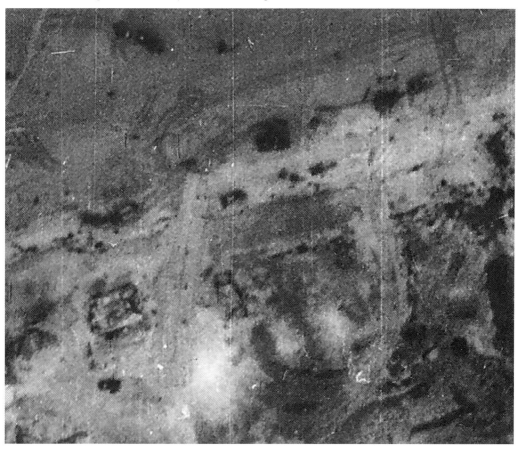

Sword was defended by a single 88mm gun, eight 50mm anti-tank guns and four 75mm artillery pieces in well prepared defense positions, most based on pre-existing buildings. Those defenses were causing damage while invasion boats were still short of grounding (89 landing craft were destroyed by shore fire and mines). Defenses eventually caused 683 casualties but were quickly suppressed as 25,000 British troops broke through the Atlantic Wall and surged four miles inland before hastily cobbled together German resistance and counter-attacks began to slow offensive momentum.

Below, Sword Area, 'Queen Green,' about 3000 feet east of Lion-sur-Mer. Note multiple, low-gradient exits from the beach. The wide road on the left is now named Avenue du 6 Juin. Rows of hedgehogs and ramp obstacles can be seen as full low tide is reached. Shadows show the shapes of stranded vessels helping identify them as LCTs and one LCI (in the center).

Most of 3rd Division had already moved inland. This negative was labeled 6 June but it exactly matches the scale, contrast and beach conditions of a series marked 7 June 1944.

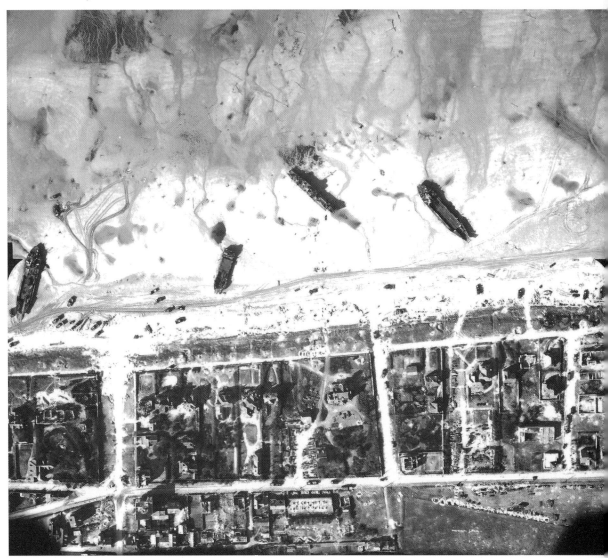

This enlargement of two probable armored vehicles 'brewed up' inland south of Sword is puzzling. A third smaller AFV (Armored Fighting Vehicle) is at right near the buildings. We see where the two vehicles entered the field. At least one other apparently maneuvered and withdrew.

An artillery or anti-tank round is going off at top center. This might be British tanks, or could document part of 21st Panzer Division's temporarily successful thrust between Sword and Juno landing areas.

The center of Lion-sur-Mer on 7 June. An outer line of well-spaced 'Belgian Gates' and inner rows of 'Czech Hedgehogs' show well against the wide expanse of sand at low tide. Only one stray landing craft gives evidence of what went on the day before: no tracks on the beach, no vehicles on the beach or streets. There are no destroyed structures, in fact some of those grand beach houses may be seen today, leading to the conclusion that either no one landed here, or the going was quite easy and war passed through the city quickly.

Below, enlargement of the row of 'Belgian Gates'. Shadows show the structure.

'Queen White' (on left) and 'Queen Red' on D+1 with the tide well out. There are few vehicles on the beach or city and little destruction in the urban area. Larger ships such as LSTs (Landing Ship Tank) able to carry more supplies in single loads are bringing in the huge amounts of bullets and beans needed to push the force south.

Enlargement of LSTs anchored (no wake) or approaching the beach. The presence of these large, vulnerable sea-going vessels near the shore indicates the threat from enemy air or artillery was considered well under control.

Below, my arrow points toward the western edge of 6th Airborne Division Landing Zone 'W,' northwest of Pegasus Bridge (adjoins photo on page 84). Discarded chutes are in the fields, vehicles are moving south on the road (south is up). Tracks show where tanks from Sword maneuvered, then raced off to the southwest without stopping. Craters show bombs mostly missing an elaborate German hill-top strong point. Trenches and gun positions appear unoccupied.

Three miles south of the beach and two miles west of the Caen Cannel was one of the few prepared positions behind the beaches. Enlargement of vertical imagery from the previous day discloses no apparent damage or occupancy of the obviously well-developed defense point on the road south to Bieville. The various nodes where trenches meet suggests an artillery position but no guns are in view.

JUNO BEACHES (NAN, MIKE, LOVE)

Despite a heavily defended coast, Canadian 3rd Infantry Division landings west of Sword were among the most successful, achieving most of their invasion objectives by sundown with relatively low casualties. The weight of this landing fell between Saint-Aubin-sur-Mer on the east and beaches just beyond Courseulles-sur-Mer on the west.

Buildings on fire at St. Aubin sur Mer were probably from pre-invasion naval bombardment. No landings occurred here, the inbound landing craft is heading for the 9th Canadian Infantry Brigade landings at Bernieres.

I see no obvious defense strong points on this enlargement but any of those buildings could have housed anti-tank and machine guns behind concrete modifications.

Bernieres-sur-Mer was the center of a two Brigade assault landing. Fires are from pre-invasion air attack and naval gunfire. Since landing craft are pushing forward and few are grounded, this is probably before 10 AM. H-Hour was 0745 and by that time many of the off-shore hazards were under water, making it impossible for engineers to clear paths. That resulted in higher losses (90 landing craft) during landings. However, the Juno beaches were some of the easiest to exit with few seawalls and no cliffs to scale, so the Canadians made excellent progress, storming strong points, pushing inland, quickly linking with British units on their right (Gold Beach), but failing to link with Sword landings on their left.

Below are 'Nan White' (on the left) and 'Nan Green'. This photo was taken by a hand-held camera shooting out the window of a transport-type aircraft flying west well off-shore. We see urban development on the shore and flat, open country just beyond.

Right, from the same photo series/ source, but not necessarily the same landing or time. This is not the same location as above, but probably nearby. That AFV at right looks like a self-propelled artillery gun.

Landing on 'Nan White'. The bicycles were a surprise to me. I understand bikes also landed on Sword and Gold, and soon littered the French countryside as troops found them useless.

More of the coastal fly-by. Courseulles-sur-Mer is two miles west of Bernieres. Here too were easily handled beach gradients and exits, and open country just behind the beach. Just left of here was one of the strongest defense points encountered on D-Day. The Regina Rifles quickly knocked out its 88mm gun. This picture, taken near high-tide (probably about 10 AM) shows landing craft grounded on the beach and off-shore beach defenses under water (i.e., at their most dangerous).

We see one LCT has lifted off the beach in the still rising tide and is going out for another load. Choice of a landing site for 'Mike Green' requiring an immediate river crossing and marshy ground inland seems curious – but it worked. German troops here were thin on the ground but alerted since British forces had begun landing just east and west of Juno about a half hour earlier, but the Canadians were through the shore defenses quickly. Once inland, these troops turned right to link up with British landings on Gold Beaches two miles farther west.

Attackers on 'Mike Red,' just east of here, faced a high seawall and one of the most heavily prepared and defended strong points encountered on D-Day. Assault infantry took 50% losses on that beach in the first hour.

One of the keys to success on Juno was that 21 of the 29 Duplex Drive M4 'Sherman' tanks successfully swam ashore to go in with the initial landings – one Squadron arriving ahead of the Infantry. Tanks of 1st Hussars working in pairs were able to quickly suppress German strong points and allow troops to get beyond the beach where German opposition was ad hoc.

Early in the 'Nan White' landing east of Bernieres. Fires on shore are probably from naval gun fire because I see no movement off the beach at this time. At right, a cluster of vehicles is on the beach gradient. I don't see any floatation curtains so I assume these tanks 'waded' in from one of the departing LCTs. At far left, 25 LCAs are on the way in to the heaviest defended beach, passing a seemingly stalled LCT which appears to have its ramp down (too far out for 'waders', perhaps it is launching DD M4 'swimming' tanks).

Below, enlargement shows beach obstacles visible in the still rising tide.

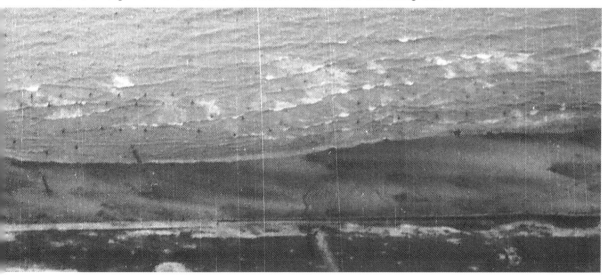

East of Bernieres, Landing Boats and LCTs. Vehicles aren't off the beach but troops on the roads leading to a German strong point show defenses have been overcome.

DD (Duplex Drive) M4 'Sherman' tank seen from the rear with its floatation curtain raised. The curtain provide sufficient displacement to permit the 30 ton tank to float ('swim' to shore) but the body of the tank was below sea level. Two propellers would drive it forward and help steering. Note the characteristic Vee nose on the lowered curtain. I would love to have found an aerial photo of one of these tanks 'swimming' toward the beach.

The DD tanks were jokingly referred to as 'Donald Ducks'.

Canadian tanks maneuvering inland through ripening fields. At least one (lower center) is obviously Duplex Drive with its floatation curtain lowered but still installed.

When I found this photo and saw the floatation curtains, I hoped it was 1st Hussars DD Shermans' cutting the Caen-Bayeux railway, the only unit to reach its D-Day objective, but the presence of ground troops (on road at bottom) suggests this is Fort Garry Horse astride the (now gone) rail line between Luc-sur-Mer and Caen. By late-afternoon these tankers would be facing a thrust to the coast between Sword and Juno landings by PzKfw IVs of 21st Panzer. Cows in the field across the tracks don't seem intimidated by the tanks.

West of Bernieres-sur-Mer, beach 'Nan Green', early in the landing. At least a dozen tanks are towing ammunition sledges. Bomb craters of three sizes in the open field may have been intended for the strong point on the left. It doesn't look like anyone has started to move inland, but the bunched-up vehicles also say there is no fighting going on right here at the moment.

Below, short vehicles are probably 'Universal Carriers' (Bren Gun Carriers). Several of the larger vehicles, probably trucks, sport an unusually large ID marking (they are long and narrow while tanks are almost square). Note the barrage balloon at left bottom.

'Nan Green' showing a little more inland, taken at the same time as the photo above. Spoil from a recently installed barbed wire line (arrows) shows around the strong point overlooking the beach. Numerous mortar rounds have gone off in the field farther south, probably the source of those grass-fires. Two bombs were well wide of the mark.

I can't be certain, but it looks like troops are on the road immediately south of the smoke.

Maneuvering armored vehicles (5 at top arrow, 9 at lower) immediately east and south of the previous photo, about 1000 feet in from the beach 'Nan White'. Even dispersal of spoil from those craters suggests they are from bombs. Different crater diameter is probably more a function of soil density than weapon size.

Juno, a little earlier in the afternoon. An LCI (center) is driving onto the beach beside two LCTs while an empty LCT (far right) works to back off. Several smaller landing craft appear stranded by the tide and abandoned. The line of vehicles heading for dry ground may be DUKW amphibious trucks. It is impossible to discern what the men on the beach are doing bunched up like that.

Beach 'Mike Green' at La Platine, just west of Courseulles-sur-Mer, probably early afternoon. Stranded landing craft show where the tide was during initial landings. To avoid crossing the River Seulles (far right), vehicles are snaking west across the beach to an exit and can be seen on both sides of the cloud cover heading south on the road to Graye-sur-Mer.

Same place, same RAF sortie, but a little farther west.

There are a lot of vehicles on that beach. Note all the artillery/mortar craters in the field at lower right indicating 'walking' fire forward ahead of troops.

Mouth of the River Seulles, Courseulles-sur-Mer beach 'Mike Red' on D+1 shows two of the 176′ x 42′ outboard powered 'Rhino Ferries' used to bring large loads from deep draft vessels onto shore. Enlargement below shows 'Czech Hedgehogs' Engineers have removed from the beach and piled at the right.

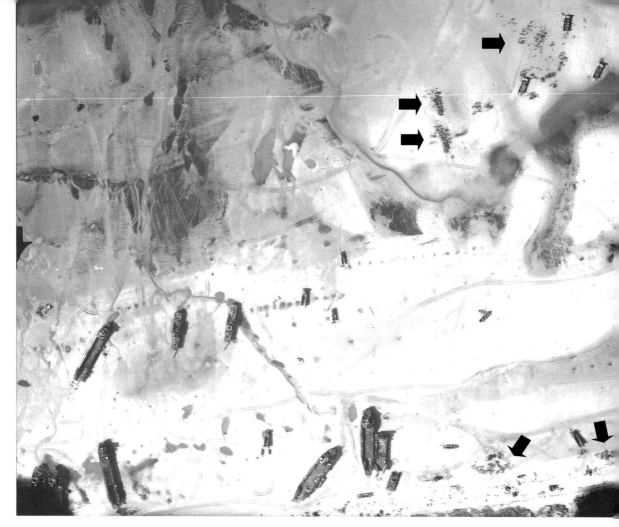

More of Courseulles on D+1. The width of the beach is amazing. Tracks show activity taking advantage of low water to clear off-shore beach of obstacles. Enlargement, below, shows piles of 'Hedgehogs' and 'Gates' (center and right) and a self-propelled jib crane (lower left) used to remove them. Here we see the difference between a 187 foot long LCT (4) at left, a 117 foot long LCT (5) beside it, and an LCM (Landing Craft Mechanized) at right.

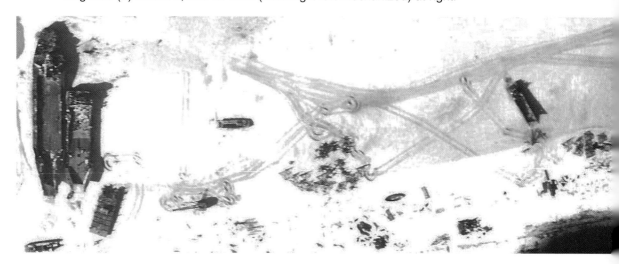

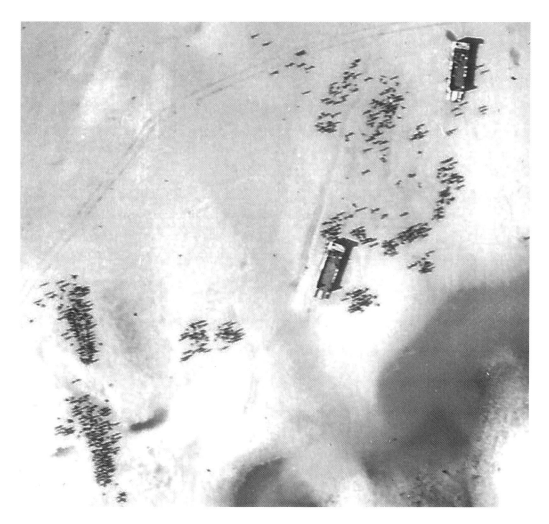

Farther out on the beach we see more LCMs and several hundred men (you don't actually see them, you see their shadows) doing…something. Possibly they are salvaging from stranded landing craft but the absence of trucks to assist them is curious. I'm stumped.

Engineers began destroying beach obstacles while Infantry were still struggling to get past German strong points. Below, 'Czech Hedgehogs' being blown up.

Low tide on Beach 'Nan Green' just east of Courseulles-sur-Mer, D+1. Engineers have been busy. Eight probable DUKWs are heading for shore. Three 'Rhino Ferries' and several landing craft are stranded until the next tide. Lower right is a railroad track heading nowhere – possibly a remnant of the old rail line that followed the coast then turned south for Caen at Luc-sur-Mer.

Despite excellent shadows on this imagery, there are no shadows showing structure in the row of 'Belgian Gates'. Blast marks show they have been destroyed, or blasted free of anchors and removed by Engineers to clear access to the shore.

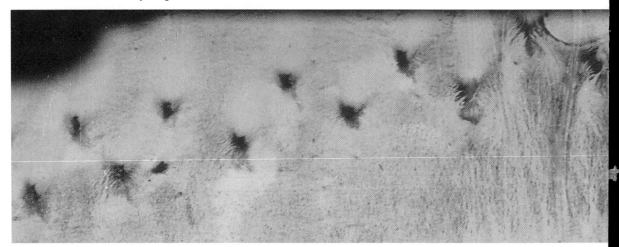

This was the most formidable strong point encountered on 6 June and on the second most heavily defended stretch of beach (right after Omaha). Those bunkers and casemates overlooking the beach housed one of the despised 88mm PaK 43/41s (the only gun on the beach M4 tank armor lost to in nearly every encounter), several 50mm anti-tank guns (which M4s handled well), several 75mm artillery pieces, mortars, machine guns and riflemen.

Lack of bomb or artillery craters indicates the bunkers and trenches of this German strong point were suppressed by out-flanking troops with satchel charges and point-blank direct fire from tanks. By the time this photo was taken, two major beach exits ran right through the German position.

Note bridges constructed over the anti-tank ditch that protected this strong point on the landward side (just going off the image at photo bottom).

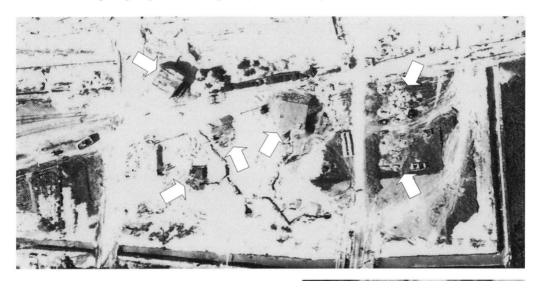

Super enlargement shows what appear to be at least three combat bridges installed, the two on the right with some sort of decking. Shadows show men standing on and near the structures.

Left, Hobart's bridging tanks which made quick work of getting over an anti-tank ditch.

123

GOLD BEACHES (KING, JIG, ITEM, HOW)

The British 50th (Northumbrian) Division, supported by 8th Armoured Brigade, landed immediately west of Juno Beaches at 0725 hours. Landing boats are seen shuttling back to the fleet or are grounded ashore and being turned broadside by the rising tide. LCTs still have their loads, and the seas are rougher than expected.

The photo **below** is 1000 feet east of the center of Mont Fleury (at the time sometimes referred to as La Riviere), the eastern edge of Gold landings. This is actually in the westernmost limits of Juno but landings apparently spilled over. The area was much less developed than today, there are few houses along the beach (one on the left side destroyed by fire) and. It is easy to see why this landing location was selected. The nearly flat beach gradient goes directly onto land above the high water line so men and vehicles can get off the beach almost anywhere and are not channeled into defenses.

The Germans had built defenses on shore in the largely open areas just behind the beaches, but nothing major. However, German troops here were on alert. American forces had begun landing roughly 14 miles farther west an hour earlier.

Landing craft are seen grounded and pushed sideways by the incoming tide and along-shore currents, an indication of why almost every landing this day naturally drifted east. These landing craft can be considered Gold Beach 'strays'. Troops landing here immediately headed west to join the major landings on 'King Red'. Small groups of Infantry can be seen on both East-West roads.

This image is literally directly left (west) of the preceding photo. It shows early landing on 'King Red' with tanks working their way inland. The center of this photo is now the site of Mont Fleury's Rue de la Mer.

The left arrow is an anti-tank ditch. Clockwise, the next two indicate bunkers, and a trench running inland. The lowest arrow shows a mine field crossing the road. Gold's 88mm gun was here in WN 33. It took out two tanks before it was silenced.

Immediately west of Mont Fleury at high tide. The road on the left is the seam between landing areas 'King Red' (on the right) and 'King Green'. We can see vehicles, probably tanks, going south on that road heading inland toward Le Bout-de-Bas. A few tanks are on the road angling from the beach east. The angling road just below the anti-tank ditch is the main route west to Asnelles/Le Hamel.

Aerial bombing has cratered the Asnelles road and a lot of open country. The apparent target will become clear in subsequent photos.

This photo shows the land imaged at lower right in the preceding frame. More vehicles are ashore on 'King Red'. Ships in the background illustrate the support power inexorably pushing the landings inland.

Enlargement of the photo above shows DD M4 tanks with their 'swimming' curtains down. The vehicle at far right is probably a 'Bobbin' tank with its roll of material already deployed. Half of the 'swimming' tanks assigned to this beach were launched late and lost nine to high water, meanwhile the rest of the 'swimmers' and regular M4s were landed directly into the shallows and drove to dry land. Shadows indicate it is still early in the morning (tanks were ashore by 0730 hours).

Note: I doubt Gold beaches got more aerial photo coverage than the others, but (without realizing it at the time) I kept more images from Gold than any other except Omaha. My British beach coverage was entirely from duplicated cut-negs (selected as important by someone in England in 1944 and sent to Washington). Most of those were from RAF missions. The U.S. beach coverage was from USAAF original negatives in roll form which enlarge much better. At the time I selected those photos, in the 1980s, I didn't recognize one beach from another, hadn't done any research in depth on the Invasion and never considered writing a book on the subject. I was only looking at the sources available to me at random, so material in this publication is what caught my eye. I got copies of photos that interested me as a PI, ones I needed to make displays to 'advertise' what was in the collection under our care. I also noted that by afternoon recon missions weren't combing parallel to the coast – they were going inland, trying to follow the southward press of the invasion.

'King Green' with surf and tanks that have just come out of water. Grass fires are probably from on-shore naval fire before the landings. A building is burning at lower left. About 20 men, with packs on the ground, are near the rightmost tank (a DD M4). Men beside the centre tank may be lowering its swim curtain.

Immediately left of the preceding images and from the same mission, this is 'King Green' three-quarters of a mile west of Mont Fleury.

Above, three tanks coming ashore, on the right a DD M4 'Sherman'. Left of it is what may be a Tank Retriever (Beach Armored Recovery Vehicle) in a Landing Craft. M4s on the left are 'waders'. A 'Dozer' (or Fascine) tank is helping what looks like a Petard Mortar tank off the loose ground. At photo bottom, a 'Bobbin' tank is waiting on the beach to deploy its matting to make the footing better for subsequent arrivals. Strung out along the beach path are at least 20 men – something a PI doesn't get to see often or this well.

Right, A 'Bobbin' tank with its reel of ten foot wide steel reinforced canvas matting.

Another enlargement of the same frame of imagery shows a bull-dozed pile of sand with 'Bobbin' material going up one side (suggesting a second 'Bobbin' load was expected). An empty 'Bobbin' tank is at lower right. Some off-shore obstacles show through the surf and DD M4s are landing. Since it is unlikely an LCT could beach with enough precision to hit that ramp, the sand was probably worked up to ease egress for an earlier landing and that LCT floated off on the rising tide.

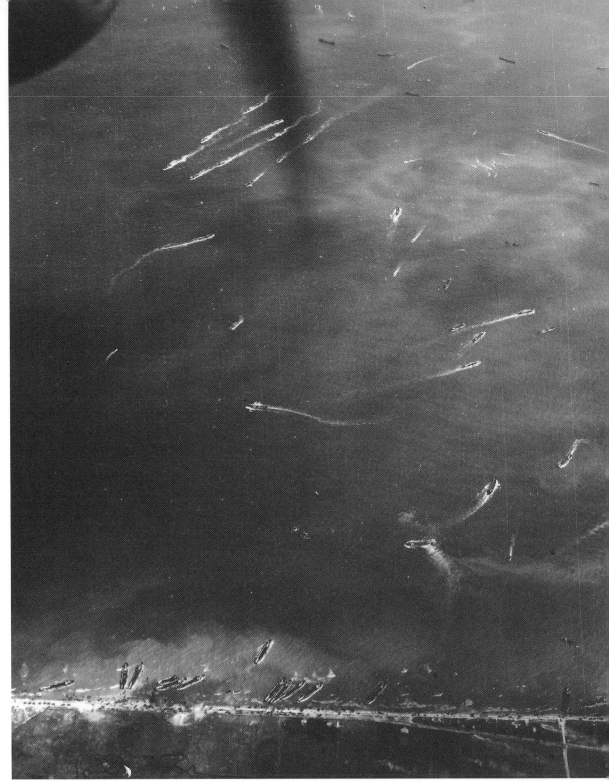

'King Green,' west of Mont Fleury. Tide is high and the narrow beach crowded. Off shore activity is impressive. The Landing craft about 130 yards off shore (lower left) and one about 500 yards off (nearer photo center) may be casualties from the first waves of landings.

The same area of Beach 'King Green' with the tide out and covering more inland. Bomb craters aiming for a target farther inland are just beyond a belt of anti-tank ditches.

Enlargement of the inland barrage balloons. They appear to be of Allied design but their presence this far inland seems curious. They also appear larger than ones over the beach (therefore closer to the camera) so perhaps they are reeled out to max-length from LCTs beached at the high-water line.

Another enlargement of the same imagery discloses Rhino Ferries, LCTs of various sizes, Higgins Boats and DUKWs like jack-straws with the tide full out. There are a few vehicles out on the sand but activity appears minimal. At around 1730 hours the war was already well inland.

Curiously, the LCT at photo center has obviously long been stranded by the receding tide with dry beach under it, but still has some of its load of vehicles on board.

Here's a look at 'King Green' about six hours earlier with the beach showing tanks landing. Enlargement discloses a long line of men trooping along the high-water line, and what may be more men wading in through the surf.

What follows are exposures from a Spitfire mission flown by 106 Group, 542 Squadron that was deemed significant enough for someone in England to select and send prints to Intelligence activities in Washington, DC.

Beach 'King Green' with standing water on the sands showing the tide is going out, making this early afternoon. Cloud cover was expanding, making navigation as well as imagery collection more difficult.

Enlargement of the lower left shows many off-shore obstacles still in place but blast marks indicating others have been destroyed. An Engineer vehicle (arrow) is working at lower left to remove obstacles like 'Czech Hedgehogs' and improve egress.

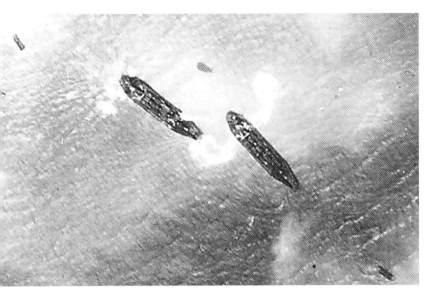

LCTs heading for the beach with LCAs ahead and behind.

The leading LCT is towing a barrage balloon (the balloon is over the bow of the trailing ship and its shadow is in the water higher in the photo.

Below is another frame from the RAF series. I didn't find negatives of the entire sortie, but frame numbers from the exposures I have show it was flown inland, coasted out and went inland again, a roaming flight indicating the airspace was less crowded in the afternoon.

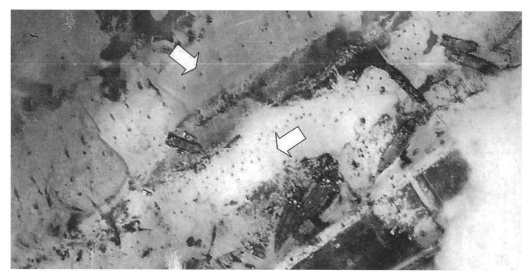

Enlargement from exposure 4072 of the RAF mission. Arrows indicate rows of intact beach obstacles.

Below, farther inland, overflying the Mont Fleury Battery was certainly an objective of this recce mission, and an RAF target just before the invasion. Bombing also took out a four gun mobile 100mm battery just south of the Mont Fleury Casemates.

The Mont Fleury Battery had four captured 122mm Russian guns but only two completed casemates. The two explosions at lower right are probably fire from HMS *Belfast*.

The Battery was quickly captured by 6th Bn Green Howards.

Below, just west of the Mont Fleury Battery, were some of the densest passive defenses to restrict transit inland that I've seen.

Arrows show mine fields as dots similar to 'Rommelspargel' but closer together. Newly turned earth shows white, and older mines inhibit grass growth with the same effect. The way these dots cross preexisting cultural patterns (fields) is another tip-off that they are land mines.

Those black circles on top of the clouds are flaws on the negative.

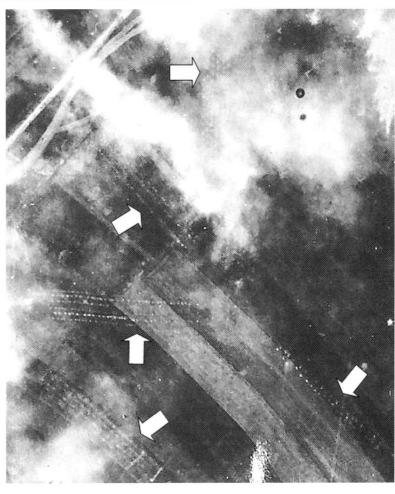

A USAAF recon mission provided a good overview of 'King Green' and inland. The road heading south from the beach has considerable traffic heading south to Le Bout-de-Bas (located at bottom). The Mont Fleury Battery is at lower center and we see that many bombs probably intended for that target dropped wide. The typical WW II answer to bombing inaccuracy was saturation of an area in hopes of actually hitting something aimed at.

At lower left is the belt of mine fields just below the anti-tank ditch and road leading west to Asnelles.

This photo falls immediately west of the preceding image and is 'King Green' on the right and Beach Gold 'Jig Red' west of the road. Contemporary maps show the area between the beach and anti-tank ditches as swamp but it doesn't look like that to me. The upper white arrows indicate incomplete anti-tank ditches. A white arrow at photo center indicates an intersection of the southbound road to Ver-sur-Mer/Le Bout-de-Haut and the east-west road from Mont Fleury to Asnelles that we will follow through the afternoon.

Black arrows show mine fields – an extension of those in the preceding photo. Apparently the Germans had identified this area a logical landing site.

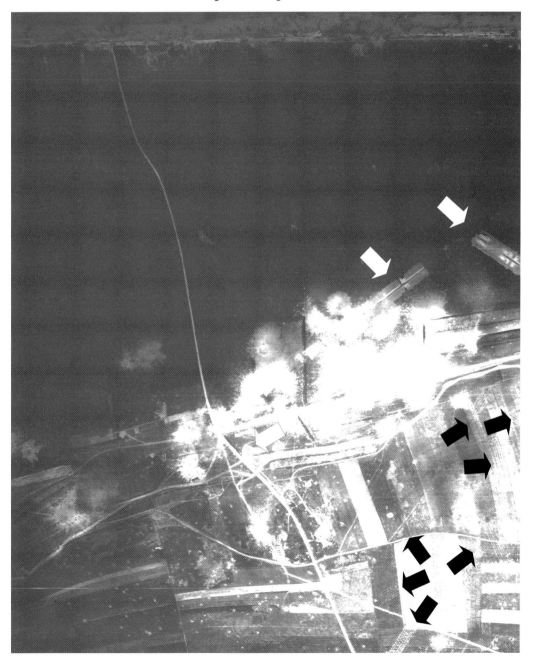

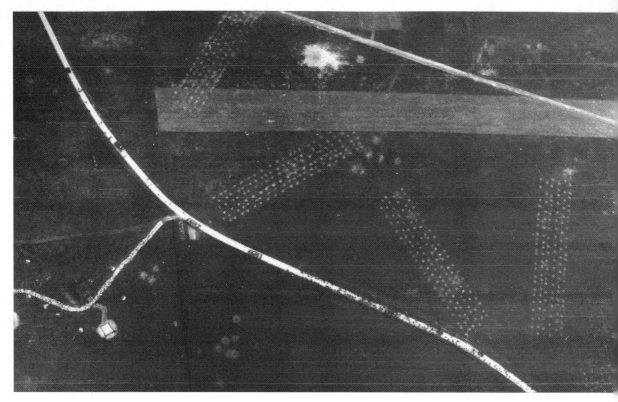

Tanks, Universal Carriers and troops passing minefields on the road south to Le Bout-de-Haut.

Enlargement shows Bren Gun Carriers towing 6 pounder Anti-Tank guns. Large earth disturbance suggests newly planted mines. Note one of the mines had detonated.

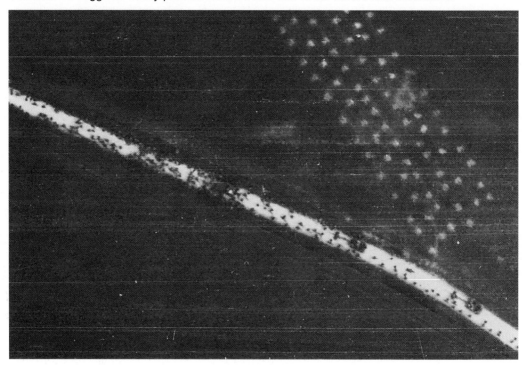

Beach 'Jig Green', a mile and a half east of Asnelles, early in the landings. Land south of the road is swamp, forcing movement on the single road.

Enlargement shows a crowd on the beach and practically commuter traffic on the road west to Asnelles, indicating combat is already well inland.

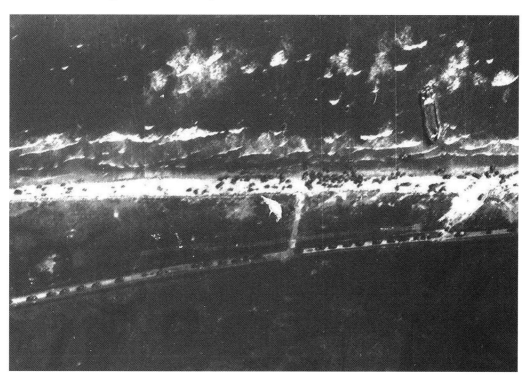

'Jig Green', two miles east of Asnelles, about mid-day. A possible minefield at lower right. Enlargement shows a variety of support vehicles, including two articulated trucks at the water's edge (semi-trailers – the only other one I saw was at Saint-Laurent). Those white rectangles at the back of the LCT may be bodies or casualties on stretchers.

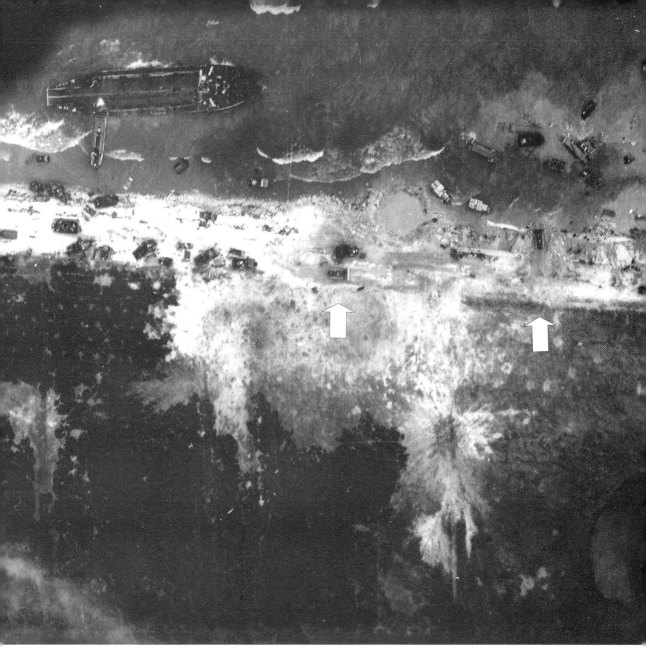

This photo is 'Jig Green', immediately left of the preceding image. A water-filled bomb crater suggests the tide is going out, making this early afternoon. Organized chaos reigns on the beach but most are support vehicles such as trucks piled with supplies – the fighting vehicles are already well inland. Bulldozers (arrows) are working to clear and shape the beach access.

Progress here was intended to be inland and circling west to take Arromanches les Baines from the landward side, move on to occupy Port-en-Bessin-Huppain, then on to link with landings on Omaha Beach.

'Jig Green', about two miles east of Asnelles, probably early in the landings. Water is high, but not yet at full tide. Arrows indicate small landing craft (LCAs or Higgins Boats) that appear to be in trouble – partially sunk, snagged in off-shore obstacles or stranded by currents turning them so they can't maneuver free.

This photo adjoins, and slightly overlaps, the preceding one to the east (right). Water depth is shown by vehicles driving toward dry land outside where the waves are breaking.

Engines still driving to hold them on the beach in shallow water, LCTs are disgorging their cargos of vehicles which then 'wade' to dry land. The rearmost LCT is still loaded but appears to be backing, perhaps to keep from grounding so far out or awaiting a slot to land.

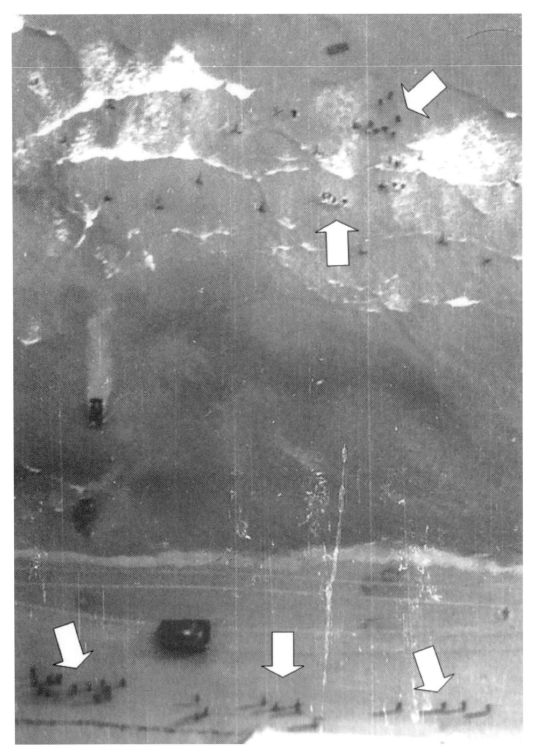

Tanks are 'wading' ashore and the arrows annotate groups of men, including some struggling through the surf past a line of beach obstacles. Long shadows from an eastern sun say this is quite early in the day.

Beach 'Jig Green' in the open coast about a mile west of Mont Fleury. The tide is almost fully out and beach contours suggest it is starting back in (making this about 1800 hours). Many landing craft are grounded from the initial assault tides. A dozen vessels still show barrage balloons (arrows), some pulled down near or onto the deck. Supply and support ships of various sizes are active, most apparently awaiting more water over the beach.

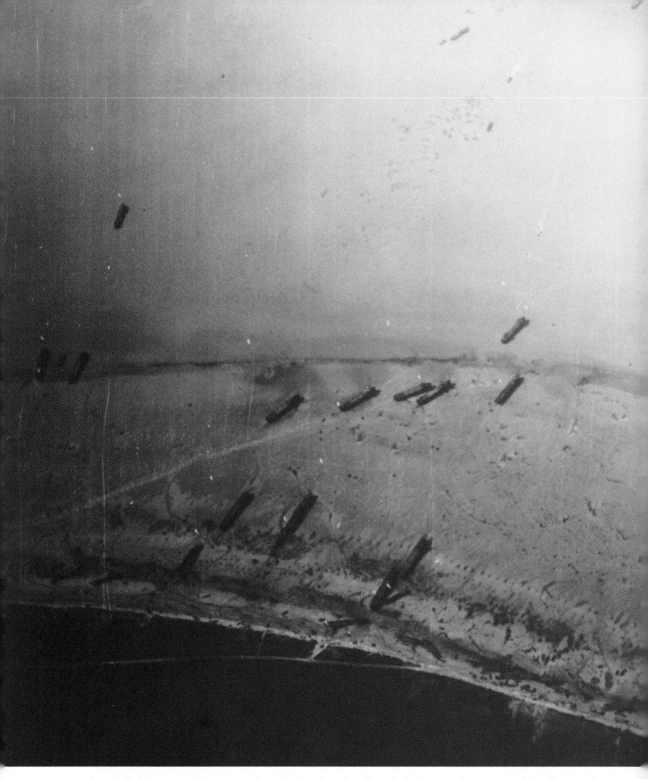

Immediately west of the preceding photo, showing the start of a small coast road leading west to Asnelles. The staggered positions of beached LCTs show landings at high, ebbing and nearly low tide.

White arrows indicate rows of intact beach obstacles the assault ships bulled through, risking hull damage. Black arrows are groups of men (there are others).

Below, same area, a little farther west. Most of these ships must have grounded shortly after noon, but barrage balloons indicate they were probably first wave for this beach.

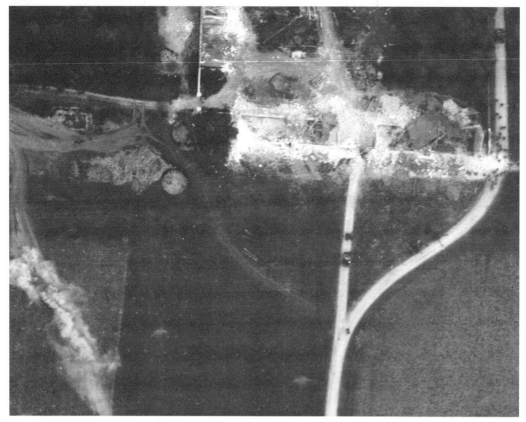

Enlargement of 'Jig Green' imagery, one half-mile east of Asnelles, just inland from a strong point with a 50mm anti-tank gun. We see a destroyed house, troops, vehicles on the road, and what seems to be a burning tank at left.

It is rare to see people on the ground and rarer still to witness combat. Super-enlargement discloses men on the road at right, some moving to the left (west). Intact roof trusses show the farm house was destroyed by blast, not fire. Perhaps it housed enemy riflemen falling back from the beach. Absent recent bomb or artillery craters, this is probably the result of direct fire or mortars (there are at least two mortar craters in the field to the south). The troops don't look like they're deployed for combat so I surmise the engagement is recently over.

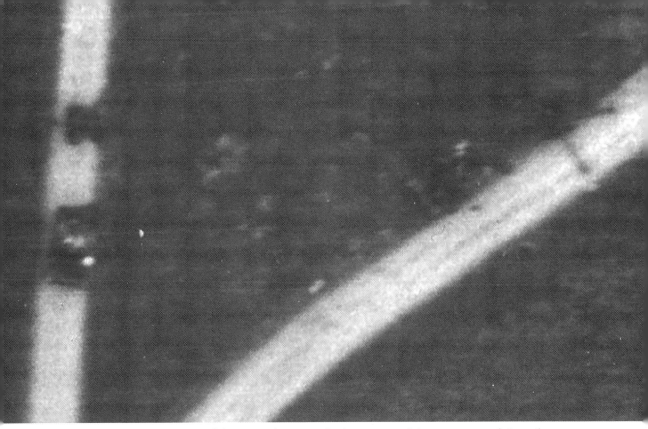

Another super-enlargement of the same imagery discloses something even more interesting. Two Universal Carriers have unlimbered their 6 pounders and both guns are deployed looking west (note positions of the shield on one and trail on the other).

A better look at that tank shows it isn't burning. It is probably a 'Flail' or 'Crab' tank working on a minefield east of Le Hamel (note white dots regularly spaced on the ground). This is the only aerial photo I've ever seen of combat de-mining activity in progress.

All but two of the Gold Beach 'Crabs' became fixed gun platforms on the beach when their tracks were blown away clearing mines, but they were instrumental in success on Gold.

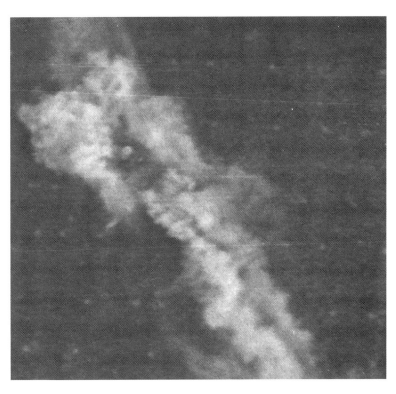

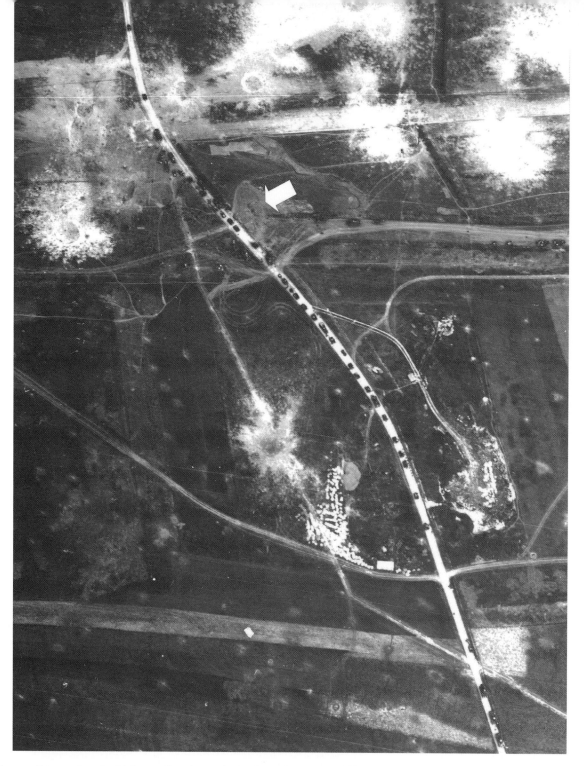

Remember that intersection (arrow) mentioned on page 143. It was empty of traffic then. Here it is again with a stream of tanks, trucks, Bren Carriers with towed artillery all heading south from 'Jig Red' toward Le Bout-de-Haute/Ver-sur-Mer. At least one stick of bombs had dropped here earlier in the day, possibly aimed at the Mont Fleury Battery.

Same intersection, only this time southbound traffic has suspended for a convoy of at least 42 Universal Carriers to slip past heading west on the road to Meuvaines.

Same road farther south at Ver-sur-Mer (photo center is 4000 feet south of the 'King Green' beach). The upper right arrow shows land mines defending southern and southwestern approaches to the Mont Fleury Battery. Upper left arrow is signs of tanks maneuvering freely toward Meuvaines. Tanks are stationary in a field the center left arrow.

Above, enlargement of armored maneuvering tracks at the upper left arrow.

Right, extensive mine fields at the upper right arrow. These formed part of the landward defenses of the Mont Fleury Battery – the densest mine fields I saw behind any D-Day beach.

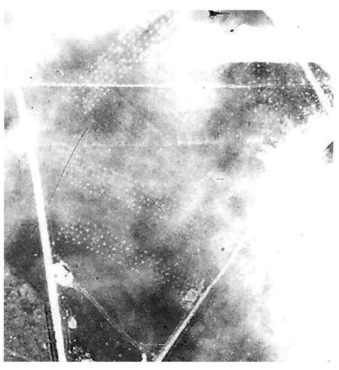

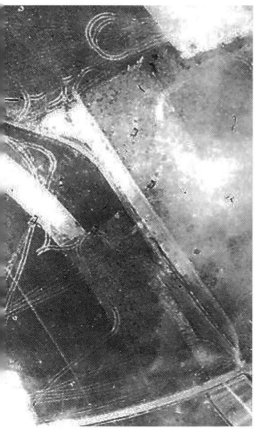

Left, enlargement of the area indicated by the center left arrow on the previous page shows at least five, perhaps six tanks facing southwest. Once behind the beach defenses and in open ground the tanks and self-propelled artillery were turned loose to excellent effect, rapidly pushing deeper into France.

159

Still with RAF 106 Group sortie 711, this is just west of Meuvaines. Signs of battle include dense mortar cratering at upper right and off-road track activity throughout the frame. A single bomb crater in a field near the east-west road suggests tactical air support.

About 60 vehicles are on the road heading west for Le Carrefour. This is inland from Arromanches, and the move will outflank 'Item' beach defenses.

Enlargement of the previous frame shows six tanks deployed just off the road and all facing in the same direction (south), suggesting positioning for a fire mission in support of advancing infantry. Four of the five tanks at bottom left face the same way, but they may still be maneuvering into position. Vehicles on the road are not taking evasive action so there is no suggestion of an enemy threat to this location.

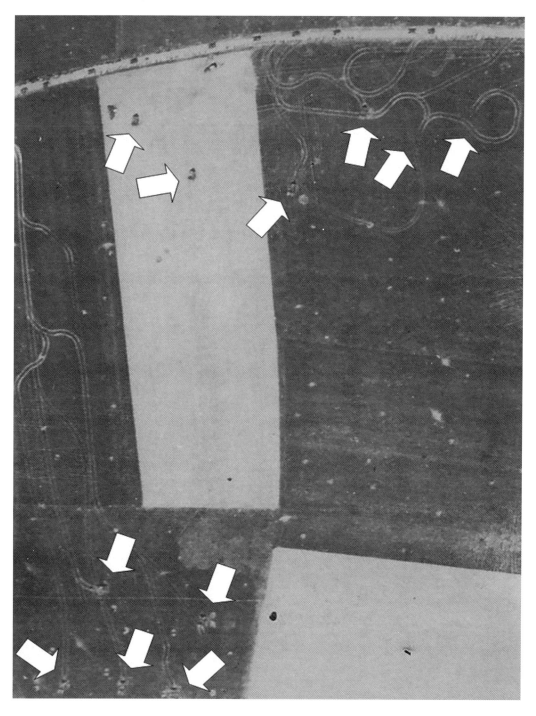

Crepon (seen at lower right) is a mile southeast of Meuvaines and two miles south of the beaches as the crow flies. Mortar craters show plenty of evidence of fighting here and tanks, probably from 'King Green', are boldly charging southwest (tracks are between my two arrows).

Enlargement of fields just above the lower arrow in the preceding photo shows considerable track activity, including the turning and circling typical of combat or threat of battle. Apparently the FEBA has moved farther south because the four tanks seen in the field (bottom center) have been going at speed, what we used to call 'hauling ass', without a pause or jog, straight southwest to the Meuvaines Road.

'Jig Red', two miles east of Asnelles. Those pits just behind the beach are too regular in spacing and size to be craters. Perhaps they are positions for riflemen – that could account for the six craters nearby.

Enlargement of LCTs and Landing Craft grounding on a rising tide just short of a band of off-shore obstacles.

Unusual track activity caught my eye. Enlarging showed M4 'Sherman' tanks seemingly milling about, then I noted the piles of similar shapes associated with individual stationary tanks. After considerable study and measurement I concluded that those objects indicated by arrows are probably the exhaust trunks used to make 'wading' tanks – perhaps removed for better rearward visibility or traverse of the main gun.

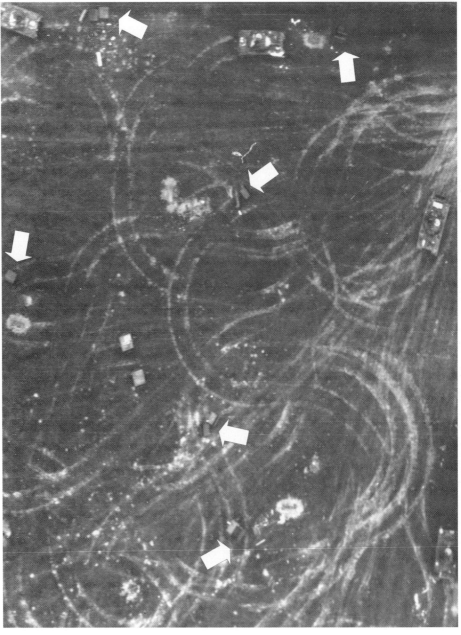

The road south from Asnelles was roughly the seam between 'Jig Green' (on the right) and 'Item Red'. There is some cratering from bombs and mortars south of the anti-tank ditch. Tracks show where tanks have maneuvered (mostly leaving the road at bottom center). Wheeled vehicles are on the road just south of the anti-tank ditch and at photo bottom. All movement seems to be to the southwest.

4051   106G. 711 6ᵗʰ JUNE '44. 7/36" 542 SQDN.

Enlargement of the previous photo shows a few small vehicles on the road but tracks show the 'big boys' have gone off to the SW. Four probable Self Propelled Artillery guns are in the field at right, aiming south (white arrows). Three AFVs (black arrows), probably tanks, face slightly differently in the adjacent field.

Below, a photo just west of the preceding imagery shows Gold Beach 'Item Red', immediately west of Asnelles. The little town of La Guerre is where the anti-tank ditch almost meets the sea road and a major artery angles inland. The winding road on the left leads to La Fontaine Saint-Come on the coast. Arromanches-les-Bains is a half-mile farther west. The tide is high and there is no sign of any landing on these beaches. There are no vehicles on the roads and, except for a few bomb or shell craters and German strong points (arrows) near the coast, everything looks deceptively peaceful.

OMAHA BEACHES (FOX, EASY, DOG, CHARLIE)

An unfortunate but necessary choice, this beach was the only viable landing site in the thirty miles of coast between Gold and Utah Beaches. It was essential that the Allies quickly get a major port to support the beachhead. Le Havre was too tough a nut to crack right off and Port-en-Bessin-Huppain (five miles west of Arromanches) and Grandcamp-Maisy (another 12 miles west) were insignificant. The target port was Cherbourg and the way to get it was for the Landings to power southwest, cutting off the Cotentin Peninsula. Two American Infantry Divisions (1st ID and 29th ID) were needed for that drive east of the Vier River to link up with Airborne landings and 4th ID troops advancing inland from Utah Beach. The French coast west of La Fontaine Saint-Come had narrow, rocky beaches and steep cliffs (100 to 180 foot) with little or no access inland, except for four and a half miles between Vierville and La Revolution – so, despite unfavorable terrain, Omaha landings were unavoidable.

The formidable task of getting inland from Omaha Beaches was made more difficult because everything that could go wrong did. The seas were much higher than expected on 6 June and particularly bad off Omaha. Seven foot waves swamped landing craft, DUKWs, and sank DD tanks trying to 'swim' to shore to suppress fire from casemates overlooking the beaches. Since Omaha was known to have the most heavily developed beach defenses, including dense off-shore obstacles, landings were planned for early in the rising tide to make them visible, but that meant troops had a long beach to cross under fire from the heights. Landings were aimed at the critical draws, avenues inland, hoping to quickly take them by storm, but currents pushed some landing craft away from their objectives so some boat-loads of men wound up well east of their objectives. That scattered and disorganized some units and upset timetables for cohesive action.

Below is Draw D1, Vierville, on 7 June. The beach is clear of vehicles and debris, but German defenses on the heights are still apparent. Beach 'Charlie' is to the left. 'Dog Green', to the right, faced a sea wall protecting the beach road. Landing as far as 300 yards out, 29th ID came under withering fire from machine guns, two 50mm AT guns and an 88mm fire from the German bunkers (arrows). Some assault units lost half their strength in minutes. The draw itself was blocked by a 100 foot long concrete wall. Tanks here were delivered directly to the beach by LCT captains sailing into heavy enemy fire, but infantry still took heavy losses, some units losing half their men. The situation worsened when attackers couldn't get off the beach and maneuver room shrank as the tide came in. Congestion forced suspension of landings at 0830 hours. Heavy fire from the heights kept Engineers from clearing the beach and carving routes inland until later in the day.

Infantry finally scaled the heights between draws, flanking German strong points and opening the draw. Tanks were moving inland here by 1100 hours. The village of Vierville, on high ground above the draw, was occupied by nightfall.

The coast road seen at right ran to Saint-Laurent, creating a wall that had to be breached to get off the beach anywhere along that coast.

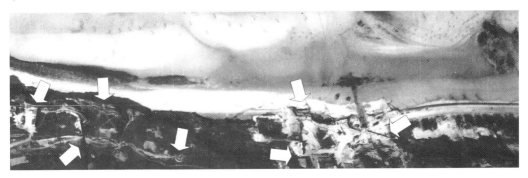

Draw D1 (Vierville) with a receding tide on D+1. Off shore defenses are still largely intact and landing emphasis has clearly already shifted east (to the right) to the growing 'Mulberry A' artificial harbor at Saint-Laurent (Draw E1).

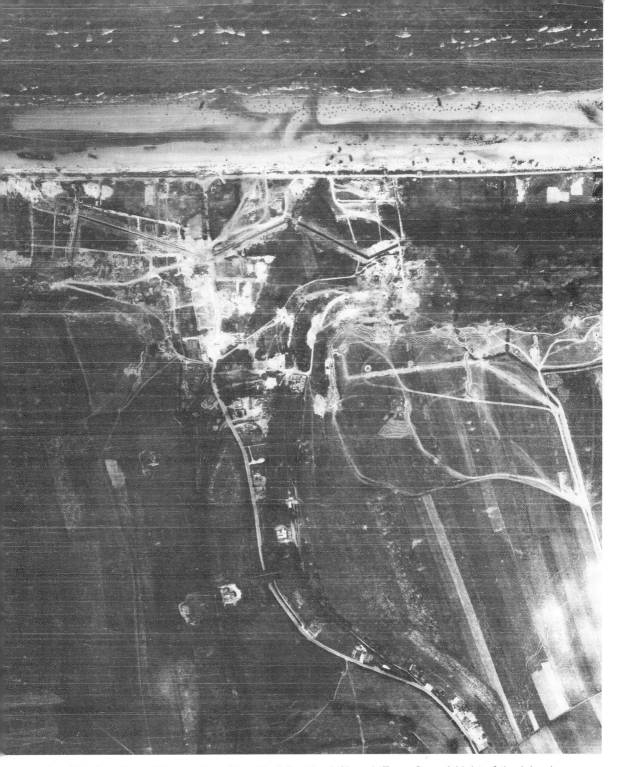

Les Moulins, Draw D3, beaches 'Dog Red' (on the left) and 'Easy Green' (right of the inland road). Ebbing tide and landing craft at right high on the beach makes this early afternoon on 6 June. The anti-tank ditch is intended to stall attacks in fields of fire from strong points on the heights on either side of the road inland.

Enlargement shows Draw D3 had a wide mouth, making it harder to defend so defenses were built to deny access rather than channel it. Bare bluffs gave the defenders a clean-slate for building bunkers and casemates, and they made the most of it. Roads and trenches at lower left and right are on the heights, both armed with numerous machine-guns and at least two 50mm anti-tank guns. The anti-tank ditch and forward firing positions closer to beach are 85 to 100 feet below those two strong points on flat land between the bluffs and the high-water line. The switch-back road going up the bluffs to the strong point on the left gives an idea of how steep they are. Strong points (left, right, and bottom) were ringed by barbed wire and the beaches were mined. Bombing and fire from heavy guns off-shore don't appear to have hit either of the strong points on the heights or just beyond the beach. Naval gun fire before the landings did start grass fires and that smoke partially blinded some gunners on shore, sparing men struggling through on-coming tide for dry land.

Engineer bulldozers (probably blades on M4s) have filled the anti-tank ditch at the road. A few vehicles are on the roads paralleling the ditch and beach (on the left), and three or four are moving inland just beyond the beach, but it doesn't appear anything has made it up the draw to high ground as yet.

Enlargement of the 'Easy Green' beach discloses landing craft hung up on obstacles and stranded by a receding tide. Particularly densely placed off shore obstacles show well and clearly none of the landing craft made it to the high water line. Ramps and mines at the water's edge are backed by a dense line of what are probably 'Czech Hedgehogs'. There don't appear to be any off-shore obstructions between the Hedgehogs and the coast road and freely moving vehicles suggest no beach mining.

Image quality isn't good enough for positive identification of all vehicles on the beach but some may be DUKWs. 'Skid turns' and turning radii show most are tracked vehicles, probably tanks and SPs (Self Propelled Guns).

Tanks and men on 'Easy Green' east of Draw D3 to E1 (Saint-Laurent) and the western end of 'Easy Red'.

All that off-shore debris is probably landing craft wreckage hung up on lines of uncleared beach obstacles.

I wish this image would hold together for an enlargement, but it won't.

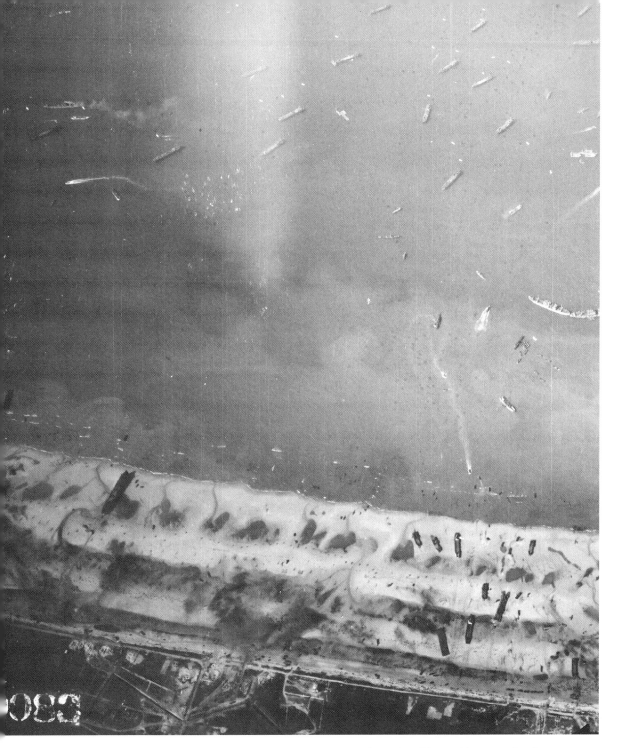

Les Moulins on D+1. Most of the off-shore obstacles appear cleared, evidenced by many landing craft going high on the beach when the tide was in. Some of those large cargo vessels must be almost touching bottom to get closer. Farther out, note the large number of ships still towing barrage balloons to keep any attacking aircraft from a low pass (a totally unnecessary precaution as it turned out).

This photo is immediately right (east) of the preceding one and covers the rest of 'Easy Green', also giving an idea of the scope of naval effort off Omaha.

Enlargement of the 7 June photo **above**. Three Rhino Ferries are high on the beach along with LCTs and troops. Trucks are off-loading supplies for transfer to dumps inland.

Left, far west end of 'Easy Red'. Lines of ramps and 'Czech Hedgehogs' are well demarcated. Troops are clustered near the high-water mark but you can see how much open beach they had to cross to reach what scant shelter there was on invasion morning.

Three LCTs and an LCI unloading just west of Saint-Laurent. The beach is dotted with bodies but don't be fooled by beach obstacles. As the inset shows, barrier ramps and their shadow make a 'Vee' showing height (two on right) where probable bodies (two on left) do not. The black scatter marks at bottom left are probably the results of Engineers blowing beach obstacles.

'Easy Red', west of Saint-Laurent Draw, with several types of vehicle 'wading' ashore, passing what bodies or prone men on the beach. I can't explain troops bunched at the water line. Upper right is probably a bridging tank coming through the shallow water.

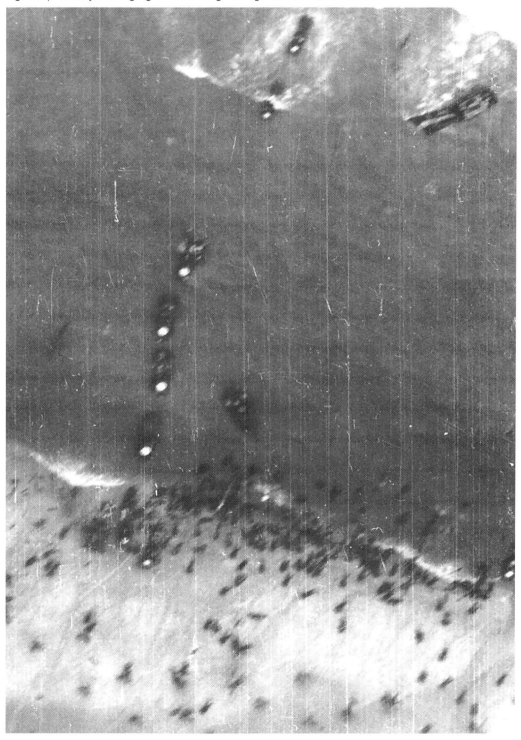

Moving east toward Saint-Laurent Draw (E1), sometimes called La Sapiniere. This is the western side of 'Easy Red'. Landing was by 16th Regimental Combat Team (RCT) of 1st ID augmented by two 'stray' boatloads from 29th ID beaches who were supposed to land a mile farther west.

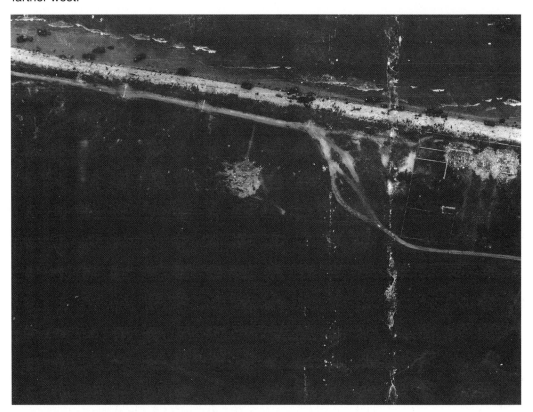

Enlargement **below** shows troops and casualties on the beach along with trucks, jeeps, what looks like an M7 'Priest' self-propelled 105mm howitzer on the left – but no tanks. This photo is near high tide and maneuver room is severely restricted (the beach is down to 30-35 feet wide). The west end of 'Easy Red' was a relatively good landing location with German strong points 600 yards east and west having poor angles of fire on this beach. Troops here were through the defense line, up the bluffs and moving inland by 0900 hours.

An anti-tank ditch spanned the wide mouth of Saint-Laurent Draw. As you can see, behind the hard shell of Atlantic Wall coastal defenses, there were no prepared positions to contend with and terrain was open for maneuvering troops and tanks. Once American armored forces reached the high ground it was 'Powder River, let 'er buck'.

Troops on the beach even with the western end of the Saint-Laurent anti-tank ditch proves some landings were somewhat west of what many histories indicate. It appears the ditch is watered, making it more of a barrier to infantry.

Enlargement shows troops, KIAs laid on the sand, trucks, DUKWs, jeeps, half-tracks, and an ambulance (big cross on large white panel, driving onto the beach near a stranded Higgins Boat). There's only one vehicle down there that I'd call a tank. It is seventh in from the left, the only vehicle facing directly inland. A possible articulated truck is just offshore at photo centre.

Following the anti-tank ditch east, the Saint-Laurent Draw road runs off the bottom of this photo. WN 65 casemates on higher ground just south of the ditch held two 50mm anti-tank guns and a 75mm howitzer. Trench lines just off the beach were protected by mines and barbed-wire. This is where the pre-landing loss of those twenty-seven 75mm guns in the sunk M4 DD tanks was felt most.

A companion strong point immediately east of the road was still under construction.

Saint-Laurent Draw with its inland road crossing the anti-tank ditch. Tide is well in so this is probably four to five hours after initial landing. By this time troops just east of here had scaled the bluffs and taken these strong points from the rear, eliminating the anti-tank gun fire, but hadn't yet suppressed all resistance.

Casualties laid out on the beach.

Another enlargement from the same imagery left.

At least one tank or half-track (lower black arrow) has proceeded inland to a position just past one of the anti-tank gun positions (white arrow), but appears to be on fire. If that is a tank, it's an Engineer Tank with dozer blade. Dark blobs scattered on the road and behind walls are supporting infantry (upper black arrows).

Note that a concrete wall shielding the gun position from the sea limits fire perpendicular to, or from, the beach. That gun couldn't engage a tank on the road until the AFV was across the anti-tank ditch.

Eastern end of the Saint-Laurent Draw defenses. This area is the traditional site of the main 1st ID landing. Three LCIs are bringing reinforcements to 'Easy Red'. Large, more vulnerable, ships like this coming in together suggests this is the Second Wave, or later.

It looks like the anti-tank ditch is watered to the end to double as an anti-personnel barrier.

I'd had the imagery since 1982 but first looked at it under high magnification while putting this book together. I saw something that surprised and delighted me – something I'd never seen before on aerial imagery.

Those are infantry troops surging inland from the beach, skirting the anti-tank ditch, hundreds of them. Note how they are moving in a general advance on the top of the photo (over flat land below the bluffs), and in single files following trails at the photo bottom. That shows where the bluffs begin to get steeper.

Continuation of the photo on previous page. Topping the bluff, single file troops fanned out to a broad front to take Widerstandsnests from the rear and open draws. It's amazing the imagery 'held together' to enlarge like this. Troops may be 'E' Co., 116th Inf., 1,000 yards east of where they were supposed to land.

East of Saint-Laurent Draw bulldozer tanks have cut their own beach exit.

This is a good overview of the land between Saint-Laurent and Colleville. The photo shows the Omaha Gooseberry being assembled so it probably dates from 7 or 8 June.

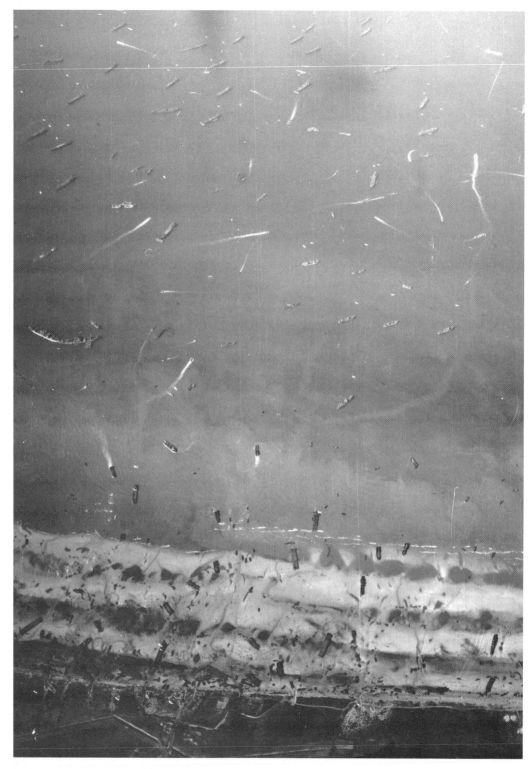

Intense activity at Saint-Laurent Draw on D+1. 'Mulberry A' would be constructed here over the next few days.

Ships on the left are supporting Saint-Laurent landings. Those on the right are for Colleville Draw landings. Troops landing between Saint-Laurent and Colleville Draws, elements of the 16th RCT, were out of the best lines of machine-gun and small arms fire from strong points at either draw, but they had no place for their vehicles to go inland because of the bluffs and lack of roads paralleling the shore.

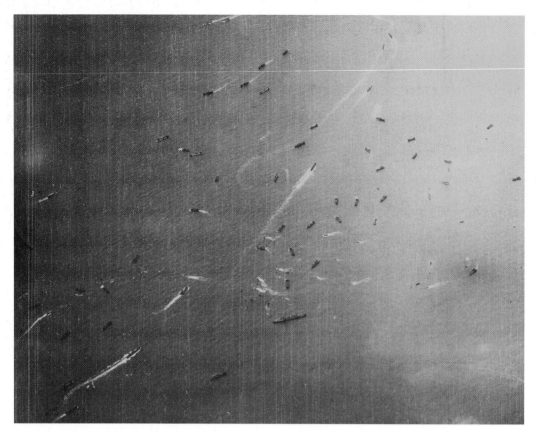

Above, a USAAF F-5 over Colleville Draw looked at ships working off Saint-Laurent. Lack of tank gun direct fire to suppress defenses prompted intrepid Destroyer captains to move so close to shore some were scraping bottom as they laid their guns on German casemates and bunkers for line-of-sight fire, probably saving at least one beachhead (USS *Corry* was lost to shore fire during those engagements).

Enlargement Below, a '*Gleaves* class' Destroyer with four 5″ turrets turned to 'Fox Green'.

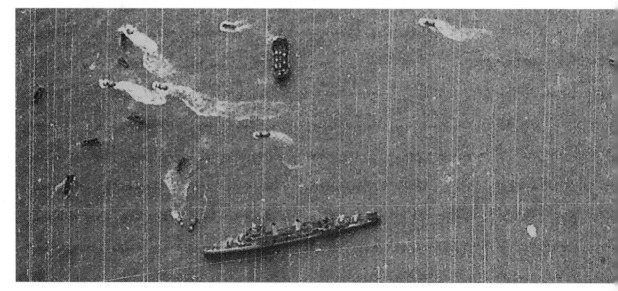

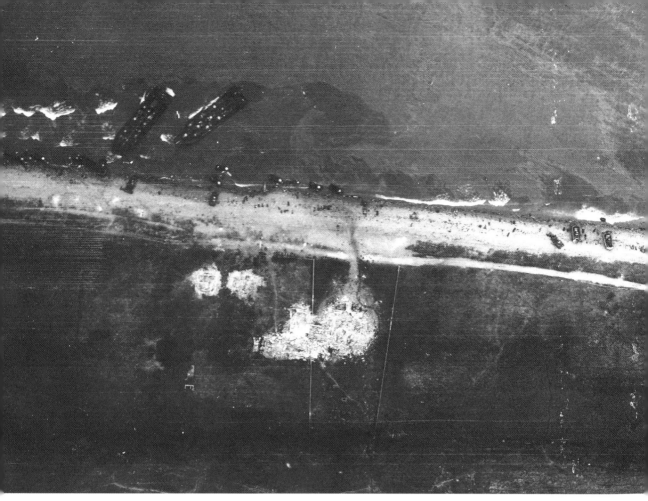

Above, half way between Saint-Laurent and Colleville Draws – Beach 'Easy Red'.

Below, enlargement of the 'Easy Red' photo above. LCTs are landing with the tide high – first off was almost always a tank. The vehicle just off the left landing craft, passing a beached Higgins Boat, is possibly a DD M4. On the beach to its right is another tank, apparently an Engineer version with a 'dozer' blade. A third tank is at the far right. Typically tanks will be seen early in the landings with their bow (best armor) facing the enemy. Tanks were finally on the beach here by 0700 hours and immediately effective in suppressing enemy strong points.

Below, another enlargement from the same imagery.

Twenty-nine M4 DD tanks of 741st Armored Battalion were put into the water to lead the way onto the beach, but they were launched too far out and seven foot seas spilled over their floatation curtains, swamping the tanks. The east end of Omaha landings paid a high price for loss of all but two of the 'swimming' tanks. These may be the two 741st Battalion survivors of the 'swim' to shore. We see them on the east end of 'Easy Red'. The left 'floatation curtain' is either damaged or in the process of being lowered. To their left is an Engineer M4 with 'wading trunks' on its rear deck and towing a trailer. Typically those trailers were loaded with Bangalore Torpedoes to blast through wire defenses.

Shapes on the beach at right are mostly casualties. Different shapes among clusters of bodies suggest people kneeling over some of them, providing care. Some of the dark shapes being washed up are pieces of debris from sunk landing craft, others are likely KIAs.

Though M4s did well suppressing fire onto the beach and clearing paths for subsequent landings, the price was high. Only five of 741st Armored's tanks were still in action on D+1.

Beach 'Fox Green,' Colleville Draw (exit E3), was defended to the west by the most formidable strong point on Omaha Beach. WN 62 was manned by the largest contingent (85 men) armed with two 75mm howitzers, two 50mm anti-tank guns, mortars and automatic weapons. Defenders were ensconced in well sited and well-constructed concrete casemates.[5] Companion strong point WN 61 was immediately east of the draw, 1000 feet away and a little farther forward to sweep the beach and beach approaches to the west with its deadly 88mm gun mounted for direct fire. The 20 men manning WN 61 also had a 50mm anti-tank gun and several machine-guns.

Starting at 0640 hours, four Companies of the 1st IDs 16th Infantry Regiment attacked directly into the teeth of these defenses – initially without armored support. They took devastating losses before reaching some shelter at the top of the shingle and under the bluffs causing the assault to temporarily stall out.

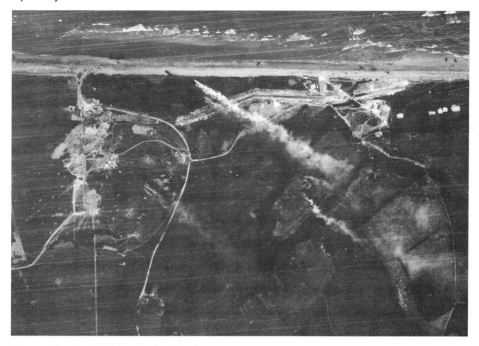

Above, Colleville Draw to Le Cavey.

After the disaster of 741st Armored Battalion's 'swimming' tank losses, the remaining tanks; 16 M4 'waders', eight Engineer 'dozers' and three DDs that couldn't be launched at sea because of a torn floatation curtain, were taken directly to the beach by their LCTs. Several tanks were quickly destroyed but their arrival began to change matters for Infantry pinned down on 'Fox Green' as the tanks suppressed fire from enemy casemates.

---

5. The huge American cemetery is on the high ground west of WN 62.

Above, the western side of 'Fox Green' (and a little of the eastern boundary of 'Easy Red'.

Troops can be seen clustered near the high water mark. The three tanks at upper left are the same ones three photos back. Another tank is a few yards east and vehicles are moving inland.

Enlargement shows what is probably an Engineer tank on fire at the start of the inland road going off the beach. A half-track is going up the E3 road.

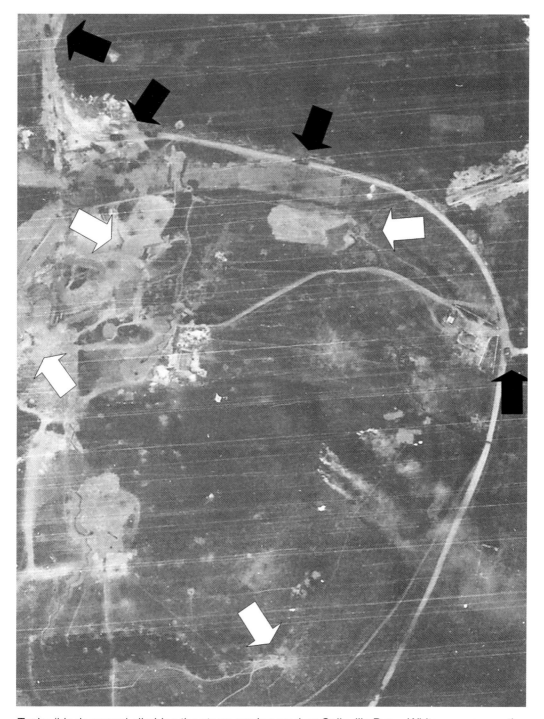

Tanks (black arrows) climbing the steep curving road up Colleville Draw. White arrows near the road are positions for 50mm anti-tank guns. White arrows at far left are unfinished casemates housing two 7.62cm field guns captured in Russia, threatening targets on 'Easy Green' and 'Dog Red' to the west (i.e., unable to fire at this landing beach). A few troops can be seen on the road at photo bottom.

Colleville Draw a little later in the day. My sense is that the tide is going out (making this after noon). Shore fires were probably from earlier combat. The troops on the beach don't seem to be in a defensive posture so fire from the strong points must have abated.

WN 62 and WN 61 were flanked and taken from the rear by 1430 hours (some sources say the positions were abandoned when the defenders ran out of ammunition).

Le Cavey (WN 61) guarding the east side of Colleville Draw, behind the anti-tank ditch but below the buffs – the only Omaha strong point not on high ground overlooking the beach. Despite manning by only 20 men, this strong point did considerable damage with its 50mm anti-tank gun (probably at lower arrow) and one of the two 88mm guns at Omaha (upper arrow). As the blast zone in front of the 88's bunker shows, the gun was sited to fire west along the beach and be relatively immune from off-shore fire. The 88mm high-velocity gun was a notorious tank killer.

I believe this is the 88mm bunker – protected from off-shore fire by concrete and earth, this gun could cover the entire beach curving away to the west.

Enlargement of the same beach shows three recently landed Engineer tanks with their trailers.

La Revolution, Draw F1. Beach 'Fox Red' was the eastern edge of Omaha (left flank). The characteristic 'fish-tailing' wake shows the incoming vessel is a Higgins Boat. It looks like a large number of troops are huddled against the cliffs. These may be elements of three 16th Infantry Companies. Men are moving inland under strong point WN 60 using the diagonalling road. Defenders likely couldn't see this movement because WN 60 was sited too far back from the lip of the bluffs – the only strong point poorly located.

Above, I'm not as sure of this enlargement as with the Saint-Laurent cover, but those dots on the road are comparable with shapes on the beach that are certainly men. If those are troops, there are over 100 of them heading southeast off the beach.

Below, three tanks on the left are Engineers with trailers. The one at far right is a 'dozer'. Failure to get tanks ashore ahead of the infantry on the 1st ID beaches resulted in German strong points remaining effective well into the morning. Pinned down on the beaches (particularly 'Fox Green') and taking brutal losses, troops finally said 'to hell with the draws' and climbed the less-defended cliffs between draws, outflanking the main German defense positions and taking them from the rear by early afternoon. When tanks got into action, the strong points were as vulnerable as on other landing beaches, falling one-by-one, but by nightfall movement inland from Omaha was still measured in yards.

La Revolution a little east of the previous imagery. Tide is full and the LCT has a tank to unload first – but no place for it to go. Two Higgins Boats from an earlier landing are beached in the surf at the right.

The cleared area of WN 60 is just showing white at lower right and some of its trenching is at bottom center. That German strong point didn't have a view of the beach and was quickly out-flanked by troops who currents swept east and landed in the 'wrong place', scaled the cliffs and moved inland. This was the first Omaha defense position to fall.

Enlargement of the LCT. I think I see 'wading' trunks sticking up on the rear deck of that M4 waiting to off-load. The left-rear vehicle may be a self-propelled gun, the rest appear to be trucks and jeeps.

This is an overview of 'Fox Red'. The German strong point is based upon that light colored, rice-shaped cleared area atop the bluffs. It was manned by 40 troops and held an anti-aircraft gun, a bunkered tank turret, mortars and a 7.62cm field gun. The two beached landing craft of the previous photo are still there (on rocks opposite the strong point), but the LCT isn't, nor are any vehicles, so this is earlier, or the LCT didn't unload here. Fires inland northwest of WN 60 (the light colored almond shape) suggest ground combat moving inland.

It appears the ships and landing craft are concerned with 'Fox Green', west of here at Colleville Draw.

La Revolution on 7 June 1944. There's the light colored shape of strong point WN 60 again. Three 'Rhino Ferries' and three LCTs, along with several landing craft, are beached in the low tide. Off shore at least 30 large vessels await unloading. The cost in casualties was high, but, like an uneven Rugby Scrum, with that sort of weight on the Allied side pushing relentlessly on shore the invasion couldn't fail.

POINTE du HOC

Four miles west of Omaha Beach, three Companies of U.S. 2nd Ranger Battalion pulled off one of the most daring and costly coups of the war. Their mission was to eliminate German observation of the landings and neutralize six large cannon thought to be on the site. Intelligence and Command elements had reports, but didn't tell the Rangers, that those guns had been moved inland (according to conventional wisdom) on 4 June, to protect them from escalating naval and aerial bombardment. This action has been told and retold in books and movies. Accepting everything said and written, here are some thoughts of an old PI and Combat Intel Analyst looking at imagery available to me.

It seems to me three U.S. Ranger Companies were sent on a mission reminiscent of the Light Brigade at Balaclava. The intrepid Rangers did what they were asked to do. They scaled sheer 100 foot cliffs under heavy fire, taking the German position on top in 30 minutes only to discover the large caliber guns they were to destroy weren't there.

Patrolling inland to control a more defensible perimeter, link with units on their left, and search for the missing guns, they discovered five large caliber artillery pieces camouflaged 'in trees' and destroyed them with thermite grenades in breaches or trunnions.

By the end of D+1 only 90 of the 225 Rangers were still available for combat.

Allied Central Interpretation Unit at Medmenham produced a graphic using reconnaissance imagery that predates bombing on 15 April 44.

This shows four large-gun positions under construction and as yet unoccupied. Within two months it was apparent that guns were installed in earthen revetments awaiting completion of their concrete casemates.

This graphic, copied through several generations, losing detail each time, doesn't hold together well enough to enlarge and look for the guns/objects present in March (when there were two more firing positions U/C).

Revetment measurements and ground information suggested the weapons were 155mm.

POINT DUE HOE
4-gun casemate Bty. u/c
G.S.G.S. 4347 - 34/18 NE - 5893
Before bombing.
A.C.I.U. Neg. Nº 62264 A

Large guns such as a 155mm could be kept on their wheeled carriages in a fortification using turntables to change azimuth. Because of the gun's trail, that required a roughly 45 foot diameter revetment that offered little protection.

I see one probable gun (lower right of the six emplacements) and two possibles (upper right sites) on 8 March imagery. There are no guns on the left and none set up in the construction area or surrounding fields and no tracks or other indications that there had ever been any. Shadows at the centers of the two revetments on the left (aiming northwest and west) disclose central mounding in each suggesting bases for turntables. Large guns were temporarily installed in those open revetments between February and March—a new battery in the heart of Overlord. A probable occupied revetment is at lower right. Another open dirt revetment above it is possibly occupied and has a concrete casemate under construction beside it. Two open gun positions on the left are being dismantled to make room for casemates. Hardened firing positions at Pointe du Hoc posed a much greater threat to Overlord landings (Omaha Beach east; Utah, eight miles west).

Three long, narrow objects (black arrows) in a central area that were not there a month earlier have an overall length consistent with 155 GPFs in travel configuration. They could be the large guns parked pending completion of their casemates. White arrows indicate what could be tarps hiding guns or might simply be covering construction materials.

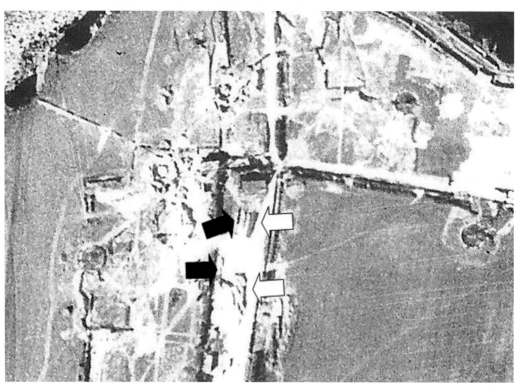

Batteries of long range guns were sited about every 20 miles along the coast, and one to four miles inland. Pointe du Hoc is uncharacteristically close to the coast and misplaced in the east-west deployment pattern—the Mont Fleury Battery was 22 miles east and Grandcamp-Maisy 2.5 miles west.

This Overlord planning document, based on 10 April 1944 imagery, shows the detailed analysis Allied PIs were doing on German defenses. Rapid progress was replacing all six open revetments with concrete casemates. April 10 imagery also resulted in bombing on 15 April. (U.S. National Archives)

Large guns available to Rommel for the West Wall were a motley assembly of captured and old weapons. In this case the guns were most likely split-trail, wheeled Canon de 155mm GPF—a WW I design.

The 1920s photo **below** is one in U.S.Army service. The GPF could throw a 95 pound high explosive round 12 miles. Some 450 of those guns were captured when the Germans invaded France in 1940. For scale, the barrel is 20 feet long.

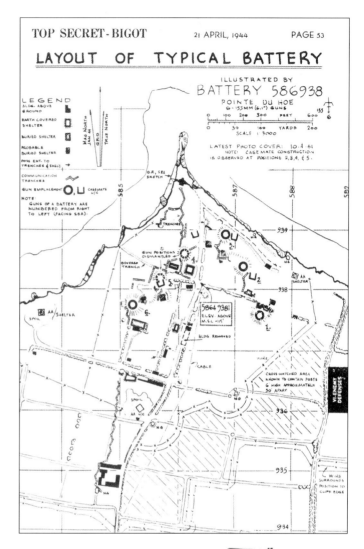

LAYOUT OF TYPICAL BATTERY

ILLUSTRATED BY
BATTERY 586938
POINTE DU HOE
6 - 155MM (6.1") GUNS

LATEST PHOTO COVER: 10.4.44
NOTE: CASEMATE CONSTRUCTION IS OBSERVED AT POSITIONS 2,3,4, & 5.

LEGEND
BLDG. ABOVE GROUND
EARTH COVERED SHELTER
BURIED SHELTER
PROBABLE BURIED SHELTER
POW ENT. TO TRENCHES & SHELT.
COMMUNICATION TRENCHES
GUN EMPLACEMENT
NOTE: GUNS OF A BATTERY ARE NUMBERED FROM RIGHT TO LEFT (FACING SEA).

Above, a WW I Manual shows a 155mm GPF with recoil mechanism disconnected, barrel slid to the rear, the trail closed and up on its limber for towing.

Planners in England deemed destruction from the 15 April bombing insufficient and another mission was laid on for 25 April.

Enlarged imagery from 9 May imagery **below** shows casemates (black arrows) and open revetments (white arrows) well covered by the second bombing. Some impacts are off target but craters are mostly concentrated on the gun positions facing northeast. One of the 155mm guns was later reported destroyed here during the first bombing.

Whatever they were, some of the possible parked artillery pieces observed in that open central area in early March are no longer present.

Three of the casemates appear near completion but none appear occupied. I believe the surviving guns, parked and/or in open revetments, were pulled south before this strike (sometime between 16 and 25 April).

Similar destruction of concrete works at V-1 Launch Sites usually resulted in relocation. But activity continued here.

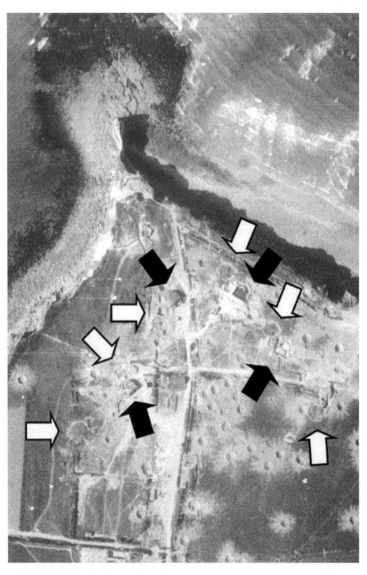

New in late April, construction at the upper arrow mimics the Pointe in a slightly smaller version of orientation to the coast, and each other. Two of the revetments appear occupied by 'something'. Were the guns taken 2,000 feet west and set up temporarily in earthen revetments pending completion of work on the casemates?

Lack of heavy track activity to the revetments suggests a decoy, and that suggests continuing interest in the Pointe.

If that's a decoy it's the dumbest one I've ever seen—way too close to the target.

In any case, PR was covering Pointe du Hoc every few days and I'm sure PIs at Medmenham were watching closely.

The lower arrow on this 9 May imagery (above) is where Rangers reported finding the big guns on 6 June, 3,500 feet south of the Pointe.

Pointe du Hoc was bombed again on 22 May, just to make sure.

Another ACIU graphic (**below**) showed results after the 22 May bombing. Again many bombs were long or wide of the mark, but this time the target, looks 'plastered' by the carpet bombing. As a general I worked for in Saigon was fond of saying, 'Quantity is quality…if you've got enough'. Open revetments are gone and all casemates are heavily damaged. Apparently that new activity to the west didn't attract any attention from the bombers. Defenders could reasonably anticipate more bombing.

Moon-like cratering made new opportunities for defenders but they also show that nothing large, or requiring a fixed firing position, could survive at Pointe du Hoc. Heavily disrupted ground made new construction, much less installing the 155s in casemates, impossible without bulldozing roads through the mess. Concrete walls and roofs would have been seriously damaged, and anything in revetments would have been destroyed.

At this point restoration of damaged hard defense works was problematic.

According to some books and websites, construction here continued right up to D-Day, but I haven't seen imagery showing new work on the casemates. The construction reported may have been a ruse, or simply restoration of the ground defenses. At least one contemporary account mentions fake guns (logs painted black), possibly intended to disguise withdrawal of the actual guns to the south—those were called 'Quaker Guns' during the American Civil War. That too could be part of a deception plan but I have seen no imagery confirming it.

I don't believe there was any heavy artillery at Pointe du Hoc after April 1944.

Pointe du Hoc was bombed twice in June just before Overlord began and bombed and shelled from off shore on D-Day. What I see tells me the report of one gun destroyed earlier is correct (thus a battery of five found on 6 June) and information that the guns were pulled out of harm's way on 4 June is wrong. They had to be gone by the second bombing.

So, we know the guns were gone, but where? Ranger After-Action Reports put the guns along a sunken road 900 feet south of the east-west Grandcamp-Vierville Road.

Five heavy weapons deployed to fire required a lot of elbow room. Typical spacing is shown in this post-war display. The near 155mm GPF cannon is in full recoil position (probably broken).

I find it hard to believe Allied PIs could have missed five deployed large artillery pieces so close to the impending invasion beaches. The big guns were heavy (40 tons for each gun and limber), so were trucks or half-tracks required to tow the guns and haul their ammunition. That would leave tracks if they left the road—and imagery before and after D-Day shows fields south of the Pointe are clear, so the guns had to be somewhere along a hard surface.

During the run-up to D-Day frequent PR and meticulous PI work were combing every inch of France for miles inland searching for V-1 launch sites and defense improvements. After the invasion, PIs found the camouflaged four gun 155 battery **below** elsewhere in Normandy without a problem. A concave arc is typical for registered artillery, allowing all guns in a battery to fire using the same azimuth data. Note easily seen tracks crossing the orchard to the guns. But maybe the Pointe guns weren't set up conventionally.

The photo **right** shows GIs on the trail of a GPF 155 set up to fire in Normandy (location and date unspecified). The gun sight appears intact so it is probably not one of the guns the Rangers disabled. This gives a better idea of how much lateral room an open gun-trail requires.

This 155mm appears elevated for direct fire, possibly as an anti-tank weapon—a function it was ill-suited for. I'd estimate a short life for the gun in that role.

Above, the same gun from the other side. This would be hard to spot from the air, but not impossible. The gate shows the gun is just off an unpaved road (foreground) on a farm lane heading through the trees.

It's unlikely positions this good would be available nearby for other guns in the battery.

The barrel is slewed to the left on its carriage and had probably last fired from that position. The weapon doesn't appear damaged so it was likely overrun or abandoned.

I find it curious that none of the reports, interviews and books dealing with finding and disabling the guns on 6 June mention the dozen trucks or prime movers required to support the 155s (if the move had been made on 4 June as reported, the vehicles would certainly have been nearby). Nor are any vehicles seen on imagery of the area. That suggests German troops Rangers saw assembling nearby on 6 June may have had nothing to do with the guns found in the trees (why wouldn't gunners assemble AT their guns?). It seems likely the guns (probably those removed from Pointe du Hoc) were hidden under the tree cover to protect them from bombing with every intention of taking them back to the Pointe when their casemates were completed/repaired. Subsequent bombing precluded that and then the invasion happened. The hidden guns may have simply been forgotten or abandoned as useless in the current crisis and confusion, the prime-movers required to move them or bring more ammunition, more urgently needed elsewhere.

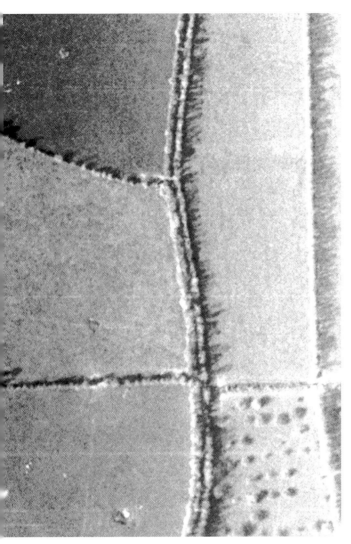

In most accounts, the guns were in trees. Some mention a 'grove' but there isn't one. Close-spaced trees line the north-south dirt sunken road and more trees separate fields. Ranger accounts say the guns were set up to fire west and with fused ammunition near (and no guard?). That would put them out of sight, directly under trees on the left side of the road, their trails spread on the packed ground. No guns are seen on 9 May imagery (**left**), but I suspect they were already there.

Disabling cannon with thermite grenades wouldn't show on imagery, but blowing the ammunition should have and I see only one possibility of that on the post invasion imagery **below**. The upper hedgerow shows two disruptions, as does the sunken road south. Someone had driven south paralleling the road and outside the trees, but the fields to the west are still clear of track activity.

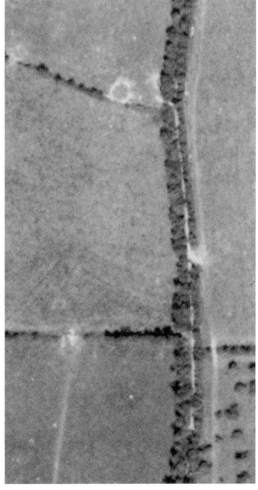

Tracks to a break in the lower hedgerow are more prominent but activity pre-dates the invasion.

If the guns were intended to fire on Utah, how would they have received needed range and azimuth data? How would they have known to aim at Utah Beach, where landings were in an isolated area and German defenses sparse?

The night of 6/7 June, Rangers held the hedge line running across this image against a German counter-attack from the lower left corner.

I have yet to see aerial photographs actually showing the guns so I can neither confirm nor deny the location and destruction of those Pointe du Hoc guns. No matter precisely where they were, five large caliber guns needed neutralization because they represented a potential threat if towed to another location in German-held territory. The Rangers took care of that.

UTAH BEACHES (UNCLE, TARE)

A three mile stretch of sand and gravel west of the Douve Estuary, and 12 miles west of Omaha, was added to the Normandy Invasion late in planning and proved to be the easiest of the five beaches. It had the most gradual gradient from low water to inland. It had the fewest cultural features to get in the way or be converted into defenses by the enemy, and there was a large portion of luck in the landings. Actual landings took place east (left on this graphic) of programmed objectives in a less developed, less defended section of the coast. One wonders why this wasn't the planned location in the first place. In any case, it was a fortunate 'mistake'.

This photo map shows where the Utah landings were intended to take place. As planned 'Tare Green,' in particular, was heading straight into a well-developed strong point defended by bunkers and anti-tank ditches.

TOP SECRET BIGOT was the security code word limiting access to Invasion planning. To see the map one had to have a Top Secret clearance, then be cleared for 'Bigot' access.

My arrow shows where the first Higgins Boats actually grounded and troops came ashore.

Unfortunately the photo map imagery isn't dated, but was likely from several months earlier. Tide height is about what was expected at H-Hour on 6 June.

Troops debarking
from a Higgins Boat
(during training).

LA MADELEINE

Enlargement of the planning photo graphic shows fields beyond the coastal roads reflecting sunlight and crossed by drainage paths, indicating standing water. South is up and the beaches themselves are off the bottom of this photo map (to keep it oriented like the previous page).

Other Utah pre-Invasion graphics show that mile-deep zone as swamp. As we shall see, in practice, tracked and wheeled vehicles managed to go inland from the invasion beach without significant difficulty.

The relatively insignificant village of La Madeleine was one of the few cultural features along the otherwise undeveloped coast. Apparently light German defenses were because they planned to flood the area behind the coast for defense if necessary.

0018

An F-5 from US 7 Photo Group photographed Utah Beach early in the invasion. The Douve Estuary is in the background. Airborne landing sites are just beyond the aircraft nacelle. A few vehicles are on the roads heading inland and some activity can be seen on the beach. Marshy ground just inland from the shore is easy to identify from light reflecting off the water. It shows why early control of the few roads leading south to dry ground was so important.

Flat bottom Higgins Boats had three small keels designed to let them ground on a beach and pull free – but that didn't provide much directional stability. A combination of smoke and explosions on shore caused some coxswains to lose orientation with the few cultural features available for orientation, and along-shore currents proved too strong for the Higgins Boats to fight. Coupled with the rising tide, currents pushed boats east. The more the Higgins bows were pointed toward objectives increasingly to the west, the more they were broadside to the current, making it a more powerful influence on their actual course.

U.S. 4th Infantry Division landed smoothly, albeit in the 'wrong' place, and swiftly overcame the sparse German defenses. Progress was immeasurably aided by 27 of 28 DD 'Shermans' making it to the beach early to take out German bunkers. Combat Engineers also got ashore in good order and immediately began clearing the beach obstacles. By dark some 23,250 men and 1700 vehicles had landed at a cost of just over 200 casualties.

The tide is ebbing so this imagery is probably from early afternoon. A few landing craft are temporarily stranded and men and vehicles can be seen on the beach. Relatively few vehicles on the beach or road running south shows of how Utah forces came ashore and how fast the front line moved inland.

Movement inland was so swift that 4th ID Infantrymen took some crossroads assigned as Airborne objectives and linked with paratroops deeper inland before the day was out.

This enlargement shows what are probably rear echelon support troops settling in. Between the arrows, and along the road, fresh-turned earth shows numerous 'fox holes', likely as protection from shelling more than worry about an enemy air threat. The five pits in a circle at lower left (with a sixth in the center) may be a light anti-aircraft gun battery. Few craters (except lower left – probably pre-invasion tactical bombing or shelling), particularly absence of craters showing mortar fire, indicates combat units breezed through here on their way inland, and there is no immediate threat to this position.

Another enlargement from the same imagery covers what I believe to be an Aid Station or Field Hospital. The upper arrow indicates three probable ambulances and my guess for the medical facility would be the long building at the lower arrow. Some of these 'fox holes' are quite large (to hold several people) and a few are open at one end. Those may have had ramps to facilitate ingress and egress for patients.

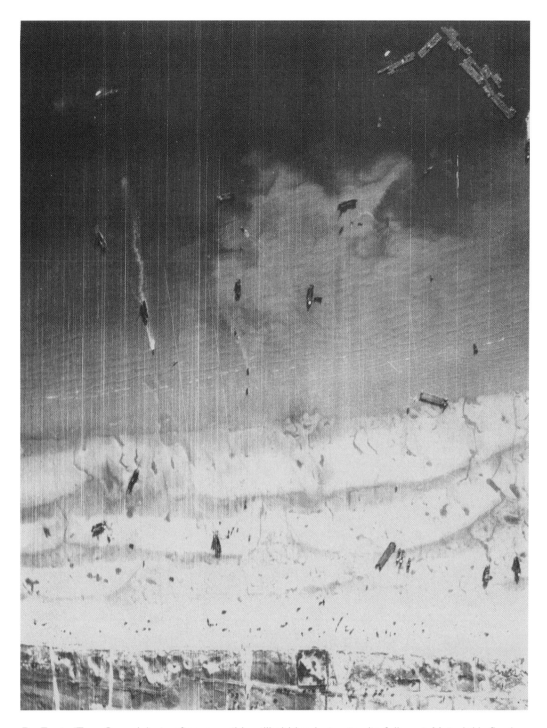

De Facto 'Tare Green'. Late afternoon, tide still ebbing but not quite fully out. Material is flowing on shore from the dozens of support craft. Upper right, three Rhino Ferries and breakwater segments are at what may be the start of the Utah Beach Gooseberry. A Rhino Ferry high on the beach at lower right indicates combat pushed the threat inland well before the tide turned around 1200 hours.

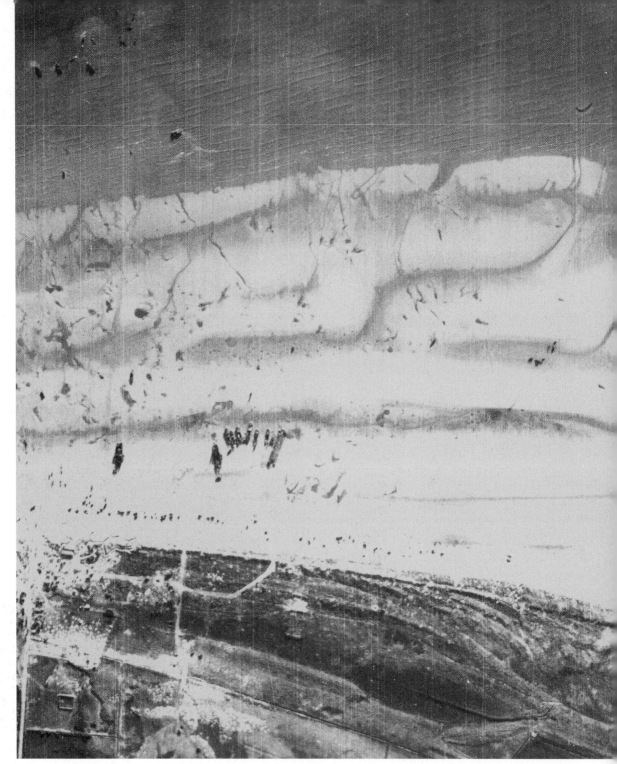

De Facto 'Uncle Red' with inland access running right through the former German strong point. This imagery is immediately east (right) of the preceding photo. To the right the beach is widening and curving into the Douve Estuary. The land east of here was even more barren and less settled with fewer roads and no defenses.

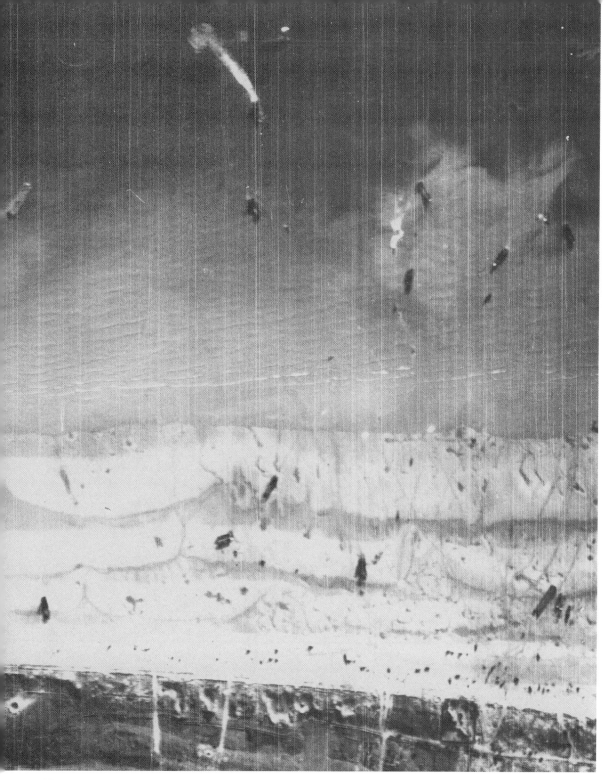

The western end of Utah Beach landings. Note the few bomb/naval gunfire craters on shore. Isn't this the ideal for an assault landing – quickly putting overwhelming numbers ashore where the defenders aren't?

Chapter VI

LATER AND INLAND

German ground reinforcement's stiffened ad hoc defenses inland, slowing Allied advances. German Naval and Air forces were unable to intervene against overwhelming Allied strength so Allied supplies and reinforcements flowed unimpeded and the beach head was assured. Meanwhile the enormous weight of men and material moving inland were irresistible if increasingly glacial.

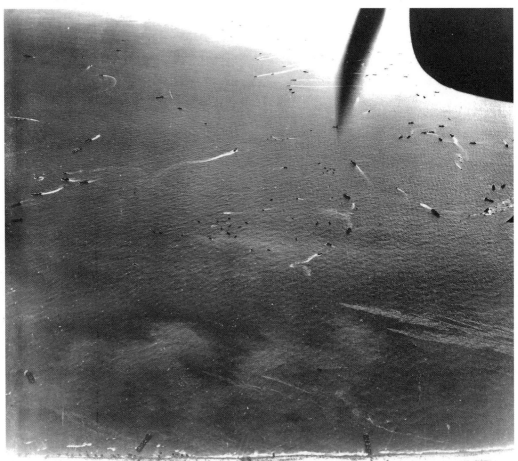

This photo from D+1 will give an idea of the continuing magnitude of Overlord. With this weight advantage, success of the Normandy Invasion was never really a question – only the cost. The tide is high and beaches seem to be working well. There is no sign of defensive posturing or maneuvering. Troops were in contact a few miles south of here, but the beaches were settling in to Logistics business as usual. Quickly and steadily moving huge amounts of resources onto the beachhead was as vital as the fighting.

From Invasion Beaches war had moved south into 'Bocage Country,' the name coming from the myriad of small groves and fields, often demarcated by stone walls laced with ancient bushes and sunken roads, making cross-country travel circuitous. This pattern of land use was particularly prevalent from Gold west to the Douve Estuary. Channeling traffic and providing countless predictable fields of fire and countless places to hide an anti-tank or heavy machine gun, this geography was ideal for defense. Allied armored force mobility was stifled by this geography and had to break out to more open land to the south.

The little town at upper right, with some bombing or artillery results just to its south, is Asnieres-en-Bessin. Omaha beach is two miles northeast. Few roads in this area were paved.

The 'Bocage' problem was recognized early in the invasion when armored vehicles were being picked off as they went down narrow lanes or rounded blind corners – worse yet, presented a vulnerable belly climbing over hedge walls. This Intelligence Report from mid-June identifies the difficulty but has no solutions. Eventually 'cutters' (saw-tooth steel prongs invented by an American soldier) were welded onto the lower bow of tanks, permitting them to bull their way through the hedges at unexpected locations – catching ambushing Germans by surprise and flanking them.

HEDGEROW COUNTRY

Normandy, with its woods, orchards, sunken roads, and thick hedgerows offered the Germans every opportunity to effectively hide their artillery pieces, and they took full advantage of it as the succeeding three reports will show.

It takes very little cover to hide a battery. Four trees are often sufficient. in Normandy, numerous orchards provided almost ideal cover. The sunken roads like the one pictured left, were used as battery sites for Howitzers. The high sides of the road, or thick hedgerows, like that shown at right, made emplacements unnecessary

Fig No.1 Sunken road

Fig. No.2 Typical hedgerow

Clues that aid in locating batteries are: (1) Zone of FA defenses, immediately to the rear of MLR. (2) Terrain that is tactically favorable, usually high ground commanding most probable routes of attack. (3) Track activity.

It must be admitted that confirmation from other ground sources is necessary for any real degree of accuracy in this type of terrain.

Three examples of batteries found in the hedgerow illustrate the difficulties of interpretation in close country of this type.

Neg. 124 FA

1806893

4

106G.770 10 JUNE 44 F/20"//S42 SQDN.←

Carpiquet Airfield, two miles west of Caen, was a D-Day objective but didn't fall until 5 July. Allied bombing prior to and during the invasion made the field unusable long before this 10 June photo. Arrows show parked planes (seven at lower left). The most obvious plane on the field is a probable Ju 52 at top center. There are at least 16 planes around the field on this imagery, most of them damaged or destroyed.

Three of the seven planes in this enlargement are clearly destroyed and one other is a probable. I doubt if any aircraft from Carpiquet bothered the invasion.

Below, Sword Area, 'Queen White' and 'Queen Red' beaches on 12 June 1944. The artificial breakwater of 'Gooseberry 5' was intended to provide quiet water for unloading deep-water cargo vessels off Ouistreham. Cargo ships sheltering inside the barrier are off-loading to craft like LCAs or Higgins Boats for delivery to the beach. The tide is well out and numerous landing ships are grounded high on the beach.

Enlargement of the Sword Beach 'Gooseberry'. Older vessels ('Corncobs') were sunk as a breakwater. The third scuttled ship from the left is French dreadnaught *Courbet* (1911). On the opposite end are two long, lean, light cruisers, HMS *Durban* (1919) and HNLMS *Sumatra* (Dutch, 1920).

Sunk here on 9 June sans boilers and guns, *Courbet* was struck by German *Neger* manned torpedoes on successive nights (15 and 16 August). The old battleship was apparently mistaken for a threat by the German Navy, or perhaps they sought to disrupt landing of supplies by attacking the 'Gooseberry'.

Ocean-going cargo ships could unload cargo and heavy equipment in the relatively calm, protected waters behind Gooseberry barriers, permitting an acceleration of the material build-up supporting combat operations. At this time, movement of supplies onshore was still every bit as vital as on 6 June. Two days before this photo was taken the first of hundreds of V-1 pulse-jet flying bombs had landed on England threatening London but also south coast ports. Those ports and associated depots and dumps were the sources of logistics for the Normandy Beachhead, adding urgency to expanding the bridgehead west (to acquire a major port) and north to take land necessary to push the new V-Weapons threat out of range of England.[6]

6. See my book *V-Weapons Hunt* for details

Rear echelon troops had created major dumps, staging and repair centers inland by 12 June as combat forces struggled to expand the beachhead. The top arrow indicates and area with pre-fabricated buildings. The left arrow points to two large artillery pieces (probably howitzers) Twin arrows show the shadows of 25 men marching on the road, with another 13 or 14 stragglers behind them.

More vehicles are at bottom center and in the space between my arrows at the top of the photo. My sense is this is somewhere behind one of the British beaches, based upon equipment and relative absence of hedgerows.

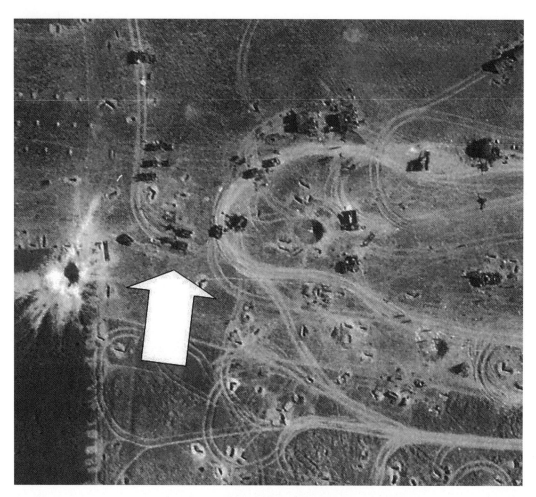

This enlargement of the artillery park held together marvelously as it went up.

There are over a hundred men on the roads on the original frame but this enlargement of marching men shown by their shadows is the sort of thing PIs like to find.

Another enlargement of the 12 June imagery. The camouflaged prefabricated structures are quite interesting and underline the amazing amount of forethought that went into Overlord. Note slit trenches and foxholes all over the place.

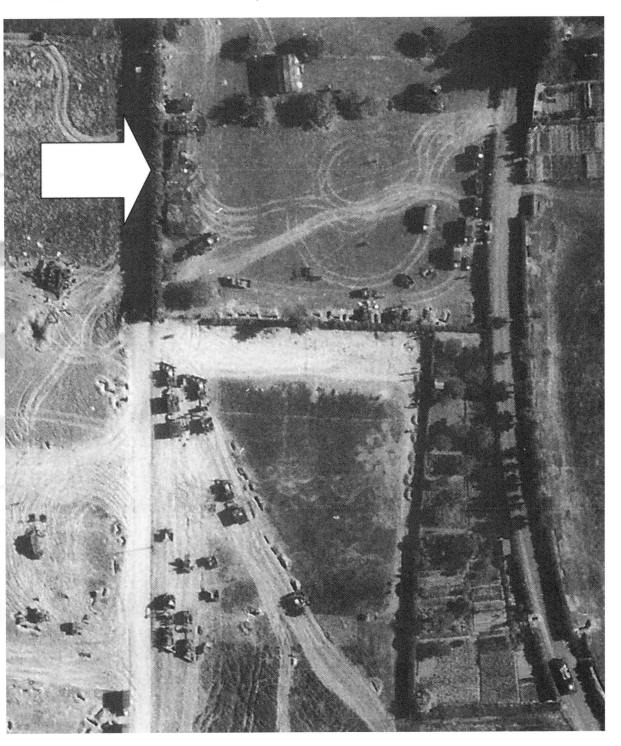

Part of the Omaha Beach Gooseberry, 15 June 1944. Ten Rhino Ferries are ready for use.

West and east sections of 'Mulberry A' Artificial Harbor at Omaha Beach on 22 June. This reconnaissance was flown immediately after a large storm of 19-22 June to document and assess damage. The storm wrecked much of the off-shore pier and floating roadways. Some of that equipment was swept away, other strewn on the beach. This disaster shifted almost all the logistic emphasis to 'Mulberry B' off Gold Beach.

'Mulberry B' at Arromanches on 22 June, showing the pier and one floating roadway in operation after the storm. A second roadway is being extended from shore. Clearly survival of this facility was critical to survival in the Normandy bridgehead. Had this port failed the Normandy Invasion would have been in more trouble than from anything the local Germans could do.

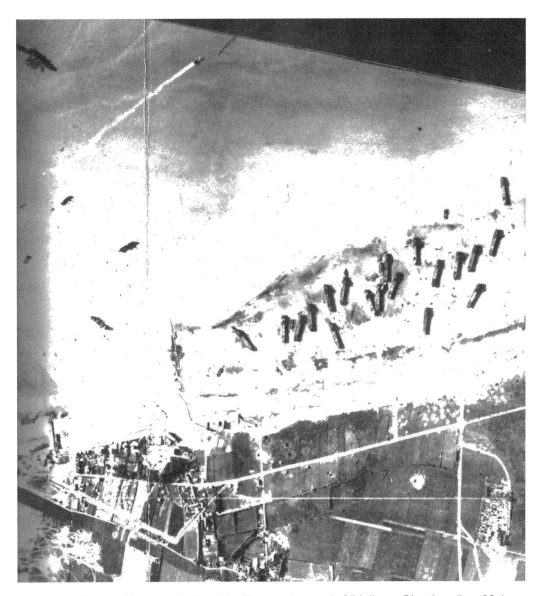

Various landing craft beached at low tide. The eastern end of 'Mulberry B' at Asnelles, 22 June 1944. Following destruction of Mulberry 'A', this pier head shouldered the load and surprised everyone with the through-put it could handle.

Cherbourg fell within days of this photo but it was weeks before the damage left by the Germans and Allied bombing could be cleared to make the port truly useable. By then the Allies had La Havre. That port was in worse shape but much closer to the front lines. Cherbourg's primary contribution was as the southern terminal for PLUTO (Pipe-Lines Under The Ocean) sending the life blood of a heavily mechanized force from the Isle of Wight to France. Thousands of tank truck convoys sped fuel forward to tanks, trucks and aircraft moving with the Front – a capability the Germans could only envy because of Allied fighter dominance of the tactical airspace.

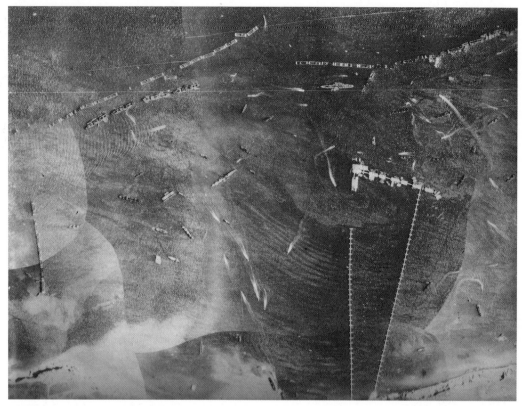

These are the right and left halves of a photo mosaic of 'Mulberry B' I made 30 years ago using 6 July imagery. Note the western floating roadway is almost to the pier head and off-shore activity appears ceaseless.

Higgins Boats and other small landing craft were unloading directly on the beach. This is high tide at Gold Beach 'Item Green' (La Fontaine Saint-Come) on 6 July.

Below, this may be the same pier seen from the ground. It appears the tide is going out – the first five pontoons are at least partly grounded. Equipment (some of it seemingly junk) on the lee side of the structure, some twisting of components and bending of the roadway line suggests this is shortly after the big storm.

A photo taken in the fall shows Omaha Beach seemingly deserted. The wreckage of 'Mulberry A' attended by just a few ships at upper right (which may actually be waiting to get into 'Mulberry B,' six miles east) but no ships are inside what is left of the Gooseberry barrier.

←NA0S Z7S//9S/ J·77·ATor 81·Sb7/b98 3068

Repeated attempts to break through German defenses on the beachhead's eastern flank were frustrated by heavy losses around Caen. Operation Goodwood (18-20 July) swept down the east side of the Orne River, finally resulting in capture of Caen. Low sun shadows from the east say this photo, just southeast of Colombelles (across the river from Caen), is from early in what some have called the largest tank battle the British Army ever fought. More than 1100 British and Canadian tanks faced over 330 German tanks.

This is what a large armored battle looks like from overhead – major bombing, heavy artillery fire, fields filled with mortar craters, and streaming tank tracks all over the place. Sometimes you can even see the AFVs themselves.

Enlargement makes it clear that these armored vehicle tracks came from the south (lower left corner) near Giberville and advanced to a hamlet on the Colombelles-Cuverville road. Direction of movement, and what is plainly tactical bombing near and on the tracks 'chasing the tanks', indicate we are looking at an advance by German armor. The turning, backing-and-filling, and sharp changes of direction are typical of an armored battle as tanks reposition to acquire a target or avoid being one. On this imagery all of the craters and destruction are from the Allies' weapons.

Apparently, heavy fire, and British/Canadian tanks driving from north to south (just off the upper right of this photo) caused these Panzers to pull back.

Adjoining the previous exposure on the left, this photo shows destruction of the Colombelles Steel Plant.[7] This is typical of what Caen looked like. Carpet bombings by RAF 'heavies' did the damage in the upper half of the image. Craters in the lower half are from tactical bombing and British artillery fire – and are directed at an armored thrust by 22nd Panzer Regiment.

---

7. For some reason, some online sites carry photos of those buildings printed backwards.

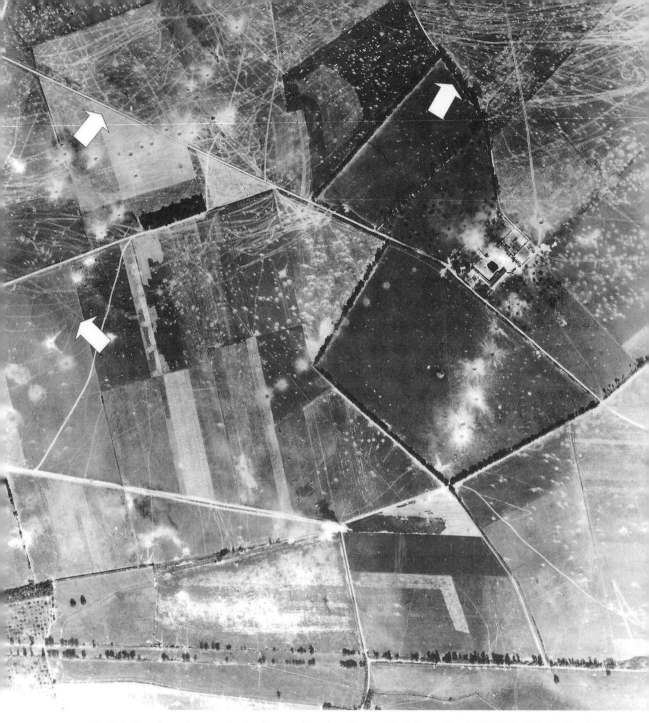

British Goodwood armor had advanced to six miles east of Caen (1 mile WNW of Emieville, I.2 miles SW of Sannerville). North is to the upper right corner of the photo. The upper right arrow indicates tracks that may be those of 3rd Royal Tank Regiment. The lower left arrow shows tracks that are probably German. Upper left arrow is the bottom of an area where several tanks were apparently destroyed.

 For scale, the two upper arrows are about 2,000 feet apart.

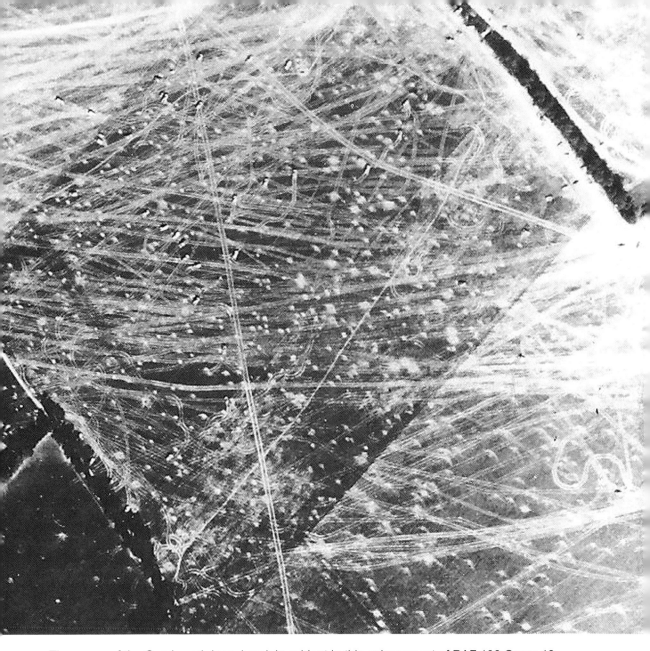

The scope of the Goodwood donnybrook is evident in this enlargement of RAF 106 Group 18 July imagery. There are at least 35 vehicles seen maneuvering (look where tracks end). Skid turns and heavy ground disruption say most of these are tanks – and this is just a piece of the photo.

It will take someone intimately familiar with the battle to tell who these are and what's going on.

Another enlargement from the same image (a little southeast of the previous enlargement) shows four, possibly six, probable tanks burning (far left center; two and a possible just above the road; and one, possibly two, at right center). It is impossible to tell whose armor is being destroyed, but the tracks seem to be coming from the south and craters seem to be chasing them, suggesting these are German. It is tempting to guess that the large vehicles (note one at upper center boldly charging straight north toward the enemy) might be Tiger tanks of 503rd Heavy Panzer Battalion, most of which were destroyed in this area on the first day of Goodwood.

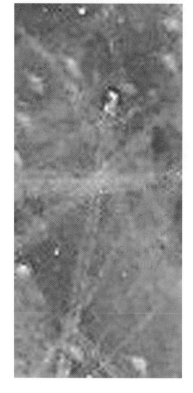

At **right**, pushing the enlargement as far as it will go still doesn't answer the question of tank ID. As PIs say, 'scale and quality preclude further interpretation'. We used to joke that it should be, 'Skill and quality preclude..'. Sometimes the answer is just beyond reach.

American forces were also pushing to expand the beachhead on the west side. Frustrated by Bocage terrain, heavy bombing was used to overwhelm the problem and crush defenses. This imagery shows carpet bombing by 'heavies' near Saint-Lo at the start of Operation Cobra to 'breakout' of the hedgerows, take the Cotentin Peninsula and out flank German defenders west of Caen and south of the beaches.

Film titling 'SAV' indicates the 25 July 1944 photo is a Strike Photo taken from a 389th Bomb Group B-24. They were dropping from 12,000 feet – clearly not too concerned about enemy AAA defenses.

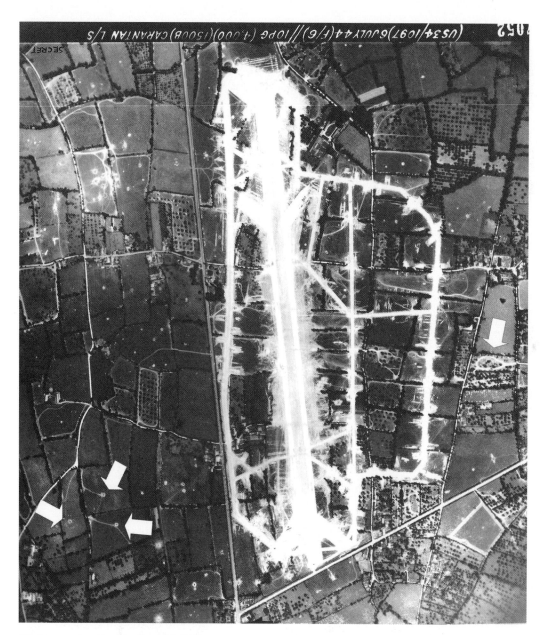

Highly responsive Tactical Air Support was a most formidable and effective weapon. After the beachhead was secured and cleared one of the first tasks for Engineers was to carve out landing strips for fighter-bombers (mainly Typhoons and P-47s) permitting faster reaction to ground combat needs, shorter flights and more of them each day. Carentan was taken on 12 June and this field, Advanced Landing Ground 'A-10'. Built just east of the city on 15 June, more evidence of the overwhelming Allied weight of men, equipment and material in Normandy.

There are at least 38 single-engine aircraft on the field, and a probable C-47 transport is visible to the naked eye just left of the bottom of the runway.

The three arrows at lower left indicate what I think is a AAA Battery defending the field. Three guns suggests heavy guns, probably 90mm.

The arrow at right appears to be a billeting area and is enlarged below.

Trucks, jeeps and foxholes indicate Spartan billeting arrangements for personnel on airfield A-10 well dispersed from the planes and runway. I think those are tents in the trees between the vehicles and the open field with foxholes.

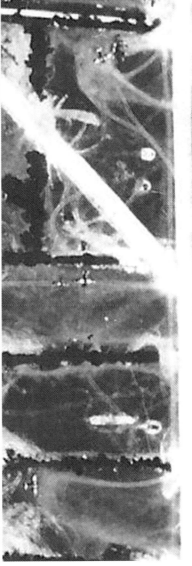

Enlargement of the 6 July photo shows the unmistakable large elliptical wing of a P-47 (there are eight of them in this image). This was temporary home for the 50th Fighter Group.

A smaller, straight-wing aircraft beside a 'Thunderbolt' at center left is probably a Stinson L-5 'Sentinel' artillery spotter high-wing monoplane.

At **left**, airfields dotting Normandy behind the beaches. Black arrows show locations of the artificial harbors.

Above, Cherbourg fell to the Allies on 26 June. When it was cleared of mines and block ships off-loading on to the beaches was less important.

Below, long range German gun twenty miles east of Ouistreham was silenced by air and its position occupied.

ONI-(Op-16-P-5)No 606- 684

PLATE 1. A railway tunnel east of PONT L'EVEQUE in which an enemy long-range gun was concealed by day, emerging at night to shell the Normandy beaches. The tunnel was effectively sealed by Typhoon bombers.

EA 12. FRANCE - CALVADOS - PONT L'EVEQUE. App. Lat. 49° 17' N. - Long. 9° 12' E.
ONI (P-5) #606-684.

Above and **below**, Le Havre (20 miles northeast of Sword Beach) was in Allied hands by mid-September, shortening sea and land supply lines to the fast-moving front and letting large ships like LSTs land supplies and reinforcements directly on shore.

At this point one could say the Normandy part of the invasion was in the past.
The die had been cast and turned up six.
Caesar would have smiled.

Chapter VII

AFTERTHOUGHTS

Unlike men, all invasion landing sites were certainly not created equal. In eight separate areas along 45 miles of Normandy's coast, over a million men went up against 380,000 defenders. Airborne landings resulted in between 1,200 and 1,500 initial casualties for each of the three Divisions involved, but Airborne/Airlanding was an inherently high risk business and high losses were expected. Many of those losses were injuries from just getting on the ground.[8] Each Allied Division landing on a beach put more than 25,000 men into France in two days for the cost of just over 630 casualties on Sword; over 1,200 on Juno; 413 on Gold; as many as 3000 on Omaha; and under 200 on Utah.[9] Omaha is the most interesting to analyze with two Infantry Divisions landing side-by-side, one experienced and the other not; one with armored support, the other not—at first. Big Red One lost 30% of its initial landing force in the first hour, including almost all the Company level leadership, finishing the day with more casualties but fewer KIAs than 29th Infantry Division coming ashore a mile west.

Each Overlord beach landing had generally the same strength and support, the same weapons and equipment. The troops were similarly trained and motivated. Why were those costs and results so different? What follows are observations (and opinions) made from a distance in time and space, and the comparative safety of my retirement home in Virginia.

PHYSICAL GEOGRAPHY

The beaches were all about the same size—four to five miles east to west. All of the beaches shared a high tidal range resulting in very broad low-tide beaches culminating in shingle at the high-water line. Soft, sodden tidal sands proved poor footing for wheeled vehicles and sloping shingle was difficult for metal treads on the tanks. Beyond the shingle, all but Omaha had relatively gradual rises inland. On beaches other than Omaha locations hundreds of yards south were just a few feet higher than the high water line. On all beaches, invasion vehicles had to cut through the immediate lip of the shore (or breakwater or coast road construction) above high water lines to get off the beach proper. Once off the beaches there were no physical features obstructing passage for 20 miles south. Inland from Sword, Gold, Juno and Utah beaches the ground was relatively level, but shadows on pre-invasion reconnaissance imagery showed Omaha with 20 to 100 yards of swale below 100 to 170-foot high bluffs, even steep cliffs in some places. There was little or no cover from the beach across the swale to the foot of those bluffs. The U.S. Army in particular was highly dependent upon vehicles and

---

8. These are the hardest to sort out. On D+1, unit reports carried 6,000 Airborne Infantrymen as missing, and bodies are occasionally still being found in the French countryside.
9. It is impossible to separate landing, post-landing and next day casualties on some Invasion Beaches. Nor is it possible on some to separate killed and wounded casualty statistics. Sources vary so I'm going with numbers that seem reasonable to me. German losses are even harder to nail down, ranging from 4,000 to as high as 9,000 men in the initial two days.

on Omaha, vehicle access to higher ground inland was channeled through five draws; ancient eroded drainage forming natural routes of various steepness leading down from the cliff tops.

CULTURAL GEOGRAPHY

Urban development was most dense on the eastern end of the Invasion (Sword Beaches), with numerous large houses and commercial structures all along the shore, and many good roads going inland. Development, paved roads and access inland were increasingly sporadic to the west. Juno and Gold beaches each had several small cities separated by generally uninhabited coast with sparse settlement more prevalent as one went west. Buildings on British beaches and Utah were oriented toward access to the sea for recreation and fishing. The only commercial accesses to the sea were at the eastern end of Sword, (Caen Canal), Courseulles-sur-Mer (on Juno), Port-en-Bessin-Huppain (a small fishing port between Gold and Omaha), and two others between Omaha and Utah. None of that sea access played a role in the initial landings.

Except for a few scattered beach houses, Omaha had little building on the shore just beyond the beaches. Urban development near Omaha was in villages located where the draws exited to high ground. Access to the sea was incidental and transportation inland was on high ground, paralleling the coast, linking farming villages. Utah Beach was almost uninhabited, having only isolated beach houses to get in the way or provide hiding places for defenders. The few settlements near Utah were 1000 to 2000 feet inland but on land barely higher than the beaches themselves. Beyond them was a wide belt of intermittent wetland.

Photo recce showed all of this. Shadows at several landing sites disclosed sea walls, retaining walls and berms inhibiting egress from the actual beaches. The western end of Omaha landings (Vierville to Les Moulins) faced eight to fifteen foot high sea walls built to protect a coast road from sea erosion. Juno landings also had seawalls to surmount at both Bernieres-sur-Mer and Courseulles-sur-Mer but troops broke through them early. Invasion planning included ways and means to breach those known high-water mark obstacles.

DEFENSES

Long and medium range German artillery was evenly dispersed along the coast, easily identified and easily neutralized. Except for a few locations behind Sword and Mont Fleury, on-shore invasion beach defenses were paper-thin (500 feet deep in most places) but, given constraints of time, manpower and resources, on most beaches they were skillfully designed and faithfully manned. At Omaha's 'Easy Red' and 'Fox Green' landings, less than 100 ill-trained defenders caused ten times their number in casualties on the beaches.[10] Once invaders punched through the outer shell, or circled behind defenses, the whole system collapsed. This leads to the conclusion that attacking directly at the strong points, particularly Omaha's infamous well-defended draws, was an unfortunate (or naïve) choice. Gold, Utah, and the way events finally played out on Omaha, showed that enduring enfilade fire and going inland *between* strong points where the defenses were weakest resulted in the best and fastest advances, and fewest casualties.

Off-shore obstacles caused a lot of pre-invasion angst, to the point of dictating the H-Hour, but weren't as effective barriers as feared. Where they held landing craft well short of the beach it cause some troops into water over their heads, and machine-gun fire swept near helpless attackers wading in surf—but men came ashore in spite of the obstacles.

All of the strong point locations were known from pre-invasion imagery. New construction was easy for PIs to identify as defenders superimposed new shapes on the existing terrain,

---

10. Two Divisions landing in four miles of beach gave the defenders a 'target rich' environment.

particularly on the western beaches and especially on Omaha. Casemates retrofitted into existing buildings, such as facing Sword Beach, were harder to identify.

Identifying bunkers and casemates was one problem, what was inside them was another question. Casemate size could suggest weapon caliber and type. Casemate location could also suggest the type of gun. Direct line-of-sight on a beach surely meant an anti-tank gun or machine guns. Prepared firing positions farther back from the beaches would be for indirect-fire weapons such as howitzers or mortars. Human-source Intelligence trickling out of France filled in some of the details, but not all.

Omaha Beach defenses were different from the other D-Day target areas in several respects. The British landings were on coasts where towns were several blocks deep. Roads leading inland were plentiful, as were roads paralleling the coast. On those beaches, strong points tended to be fortification of buildings already present. An exception was the eastern end of Sword (beach 'Roger') where much earlier bombing forced the Germans to build concrete bunkers from scratch—defenses that proved harder to neutralize. Fortifying in an urban setting somewhat limited choice of location and restricted lines of fire. Flammable construction materials in pre-existing buildings made them more vulnerable to damage from bombing, gunfire from ships and attack by tanks. With the exception of Les Moulins, villages along Omaha were on high ground and didn't overlook the beaches. Omaha defenses were built from scratch in open land, taking full advantage of the terrain, using all the engineering skill and experience from years on the Russian Front. The resulting concrete casemates and bunkers were artfully sited to withstand enemy fire from off-shore while sweeping the beaches with their own guns. Omaha strongpoints were the only defenses looking down with a commanding view of the beaches.

The key to victory, particularly on Omaha, was getting tanks ashore to take out defenses and reach maneuver ground beyond—and both sides knew it. German defenders did a masterful job of blocking Omaha's five inland access routes and turning them into killing grounds. Strong points on the heights above each draw allowed defenders to engage landing forces while well off-shore and crossing the open sands, finally raking the coastal berms with automatic weapons, heavy machine guns, mortars, anti-tank guns and light artillery. Strong points on each beach provided enfilade fire, supporting each other and punishing attackers for a considerable range east and west. Because of the concave shoreline, Omaha landings were commonly under fire from three to five strong points. Off shore obstacles were also heavy immediately opposite the five Omaha draws.

INITIAL ATTACK OPERATIONS

Pre-invasion Naval fire from heavy guns was less effective than expected, little falling on the actual beach defenses. It might have been more helpful to have a creeping barrage roll up the beach at low tide to destroy off-shore obstacles and detonate mines—much like in World War I (since Normandy was essentially a wide-front head on assault a' la the Somme). However, tearing up an urban area with large caliber fire usually does more to provide additional and unexpected defense opportunities for the enemy. The few Destroyers that dared to go in close, supporting attackers with 5″ flat-trajectory gunfire at point targets, probably saved several beaches, certainly the 1st ID end of Omaha.

Sorry airmen comrades—the same comments apply. Pre-invasion bombing of the Atlantic Wall didn't accomplish much. Perhaps the most successful was Pointe du Hoc, the most heavily bombed location by 5 June. Installation of large-bore guns was thwarted, but the site still had a vigorous small-weapons defense when the Rangers famously scaled those cliffs. However, horizontal bombing deeper inland was highly effective, cutting rail and road lines that German reinforcements needed to use, serving to isolate the beachhead. Caen's airport is an example of aerial bombardment doing its job, as was last minute bombing of the Mont Fleury Battery behind Gold beaches. But imagery says horizontal bombing was almost useless against the beach defenses. Horizontal bombing by heavy and medium bombers in WW II just didn't have the accuracy to hit small 'hard targets' like the concrete casements guarding landing beaches. Tactical fighter-bombers employing dive-bombing, rockets and strafing were extremely effective once combat had expanded beyond Atlantic Wall defenses, successfully attacking point targets as small as moving tanks, interdicting behind the FEBA and controlling the air over the battlefield.

Assault troops were basically armed with hand weapons: pistols, rifles, BAR, BREN and STEN guns, Bangalore Torpedoes, flame throwers, satchel charges, PIAT and 'Bazooka' anti-tank weapons. None of those were particularly effective against hardened casemates. Getting tanks ashore early proved a key to success on most beaches.[11] Near failure of experienced infantry without tanks on the east end of Omaha proves the point. Being cut to pieces by weapons out-ranging them, firing from emplacements they couldn't eliminate with the weapons on the beach, caused many troops to go to ground. Once even experienced troops crouch in cover during intense fire, it is hard to get them attacking again. Facing down defending machine-guns, direct fire from tank main-guns was extremely effective in suppressing fire from German anti-tank and machine-gun bunkers on every D-Day beach. Tanks on the beach also did wonders for infantry morale.

11. British beaches also had Churchill tanks called Armored Vehicle, Royal Engineers (AVRE), mounting a Petard Mortar that threw a 40 pound High Explosive charge 150 yards to reduce barricades and bunkers.

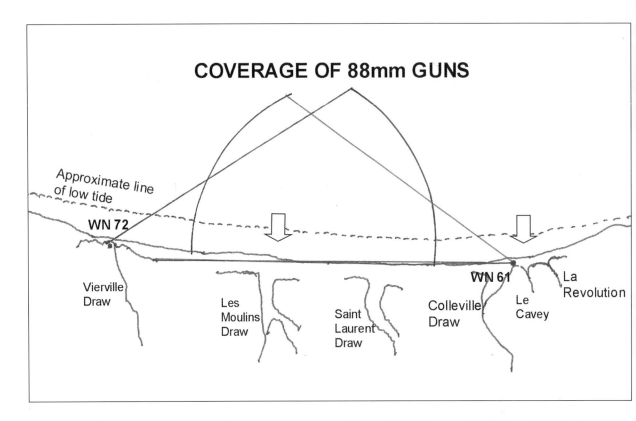

COVERAGE OF 88mm GUNS

Approximate line of low tide

WN 72

Vierville Draw

Les Moulins Draw

Saint Laurent Draw

Colleville Draw

WN 61

Le Cavey

La Revolution

German field artillery and mortars were zeroed in and sited to provide high-angle fire at beaches east and/or west of a strong point. They were effective when targets were clustered near the high-water line—less so as assault boats approached. Targets on the beaches were too mobile and too randomly positioned, German observation data too disrupted, for defending field artillery to do aimed damage on the beaches. But they did a lot until troops moved inland.

Direct fire weapons were another story. Positioned for enfilade fire, and aiming with almost flat trajectory, those weapons could engage targets off shore out to their maximum range, and they accounted for most of the landing craft casualties. The 50mm PaK 38 Anti-tank Gun had a range of 500 yards (with Armored Piercing ammunition) and maximum range of 1540 yards. An M4 tank's gun and armor were on a par with German 50mm anti-tank guns in a shoot-out. A solid hit at short range and the right angle could penetrate the M4's armor but the tank's 75mm turret gun had the advantage directly facing a casemate opening.

On 6 June the M4s were only overmatched by 88mm guns—every Invasion beach faced at least one, Sword and Omaha each had two. The 88mm had an effective range of 4,400 yards and could reach out to 17,000 yards.[12] A high-velocity anti-aircraft weapon that could throw a 20 pound round to an altitude of 25,000 feet had the punch necessary to penetrate Allied tank armor. Eighty-eights encountered in Normandy were PaK 43/41s, the AAA gun mounted low on wheels and with an armored shield for the gunners. Those were direct fire weapons, depending on line-of sight for target acquisition and firing.

The concave coastline meant the two 88s at Omaha Beach were particularly well sited to overlap coverage from the base of the bluffs to well off-shore—but not directly out to sea. Arcs show a nominal 5,000 yard range. Arrows indicate the initial assault landings.

---

12. Data well known to the Allies from combat experience and weapons captured in North Africa.

Both attackers and defenders knew the 88s were the most potent weapons in the defense mix and an old military adage is 'if the enemy is in range, so are you'. There was no escaping those guns, they had to be faced. The 88s took a toll on every beach—landing craft, tanks and riflemen. Destroying those guns was a high priority for every landing. One of the 88s on Sword destroyed four tanks and several landing craft before it was silenced. Eventually all were taken out by persistence and combined attacks from infantry and pairs of tanks working as teams to draw fire and respond. The cold truth was the Allies could keep landing more men and tanks and the defenders couldn't bring up new guns.

Where tanks on other beaches successfully engaged German strong points with nearly horizontal fire from their turret guns, the 'Shermans' may have been less effective on Omaha because many German defense positions were on 100+ foot high bluffs. Perhaps the maximum 25 degree elevation on M4 75mm guns made it harder (or slower loading) for them to aim and fire up at bunkers on the heights flanking each draw.

STRATEGY AND TACTICS

Location of the Normandy landings was a pragmatic balance between:
- Proximity to bases and ports in the UK.
- A location where the Allies could gain and maintain control of the sea and air.
- Enough space to land nine Divisions and maneuver toward meaningful goals.
- Places where defending German forces were relatively thin on the ground.
- Places where massed landing support forces would be least vulnerable.

Admittedly fire from defenses, smoke on shore, unforeseen currents and fear made it easy for coxswains to be confused and land at the wrong places, but it is curious why the criteria above wasn't applied to selection of the individual beaches themselves. Sword landings had little choice and punched straight ahead at several locations, quickly reaching metalled roads heading inland. Troops on Juno had plenty of room east-to-west and yet charged directly into the teeth of the only two really well defended nodes in that landing area—and had the second highest losses for the day. Once through the defensive crust the Canadians also had the greatest progress, achieving almost all of their D-Day objectives by nightfall. On Gold, the heaviest defensive firepower (Mont Fleury) was neutralized by bombing and sidestepped. Landing forces arriving on relatively undefended beaches withstood enfilade fire until strongpoints could be taken from the side or rear, resulting in the second fewest casualties of the day.

The same was certainly not true on Omaha—the most costly beaches. Trying to push two Divisions ashore to take the defenses by storm was brute force and very expensive before it paid off. Attacking between the infamous Draws would have meant suffering intense enfilade fire (but troops faced that anyway) and complete reliance on only Infantry weapons (but 1st ID did anyway). Attacking directly at the Draws meant going into the strength of defenses specifically designed and focused to repulse landings and deny the Draws. After hours of being pinned down and taking brutal losses, when troops scaled the heights between Draws and attacked German strong points from the flank or rear, the Widerstandsnests were quickly neutralized or abandoned. Defenders in strong points faced in a single direction and were not a mobile force. Defenders had routes for retreat but no 'fall back' positions. Requiring vehicles not immediately available for towing, defending guns couldn't be removed from casemates and used elsewhere, so why not intentionally by-pass some of them? Of course the larger weapons, including the howitzers would still have been effective against landing craft bringing in reinforcements until their casemates were eliminated or they ran out of ammunition, but I believe far fewer assault troops would have been casualties in the long run by swift inland pushes between strong points to get beyond the enfilade fire. However, that would have required landing precision probably beyond the Coxswains and conditions in the initial wave.

Utah was also planned for frontal assault on German strong points (remember Utah was added late in the planning process). By accident, units on Utah came ashore where the defenses were weak and made that landing the most successful of the five beaches. Surely that should have been a lesson for future assault planning.

Conditions in Pacific island landings were so different their lessons were of little help in Overlord planning. The only experience planners could use to design the Normandy landings were virtually unopposed landings in North Africa (a little over 1000 casualties), expensive success in Sicily (25,000 casualties) and Invasion of Italy (12,500 casualties). The January 1944 disaster at Anzio was too recent to understand what went so wrong and why. I suspect British planners were also haunted by specters of Gallipoli and Dieppe. When reports for H-Hour + 8 came in you can almost feel the sighs of relief. Rising casualties and slowing/stalling advances a week after D-Day must have given generals shivers of discomfort as they pictured another Salerno-stall out.[13]

Looking at imagery showing what was faced and the spaces involved, it is obvious that Normandy Invasion planning involved an enormous amount of detailed, sophisticated, even subtle, thinking, and the logistical arrangements were amazing. But we can also see there was little finesse in selection of the actual assault landing sites and tactics. Rather they had overtones of World War I brute force, head-on trench attacks, knowingly using sheer weight of expendable men and equipment to trump Rommel's 'stop them on the beach' strategy.

AERIAL PHOTORECONNAISSANCE COVERAGE

PR was covering what would become the OVERLORD landing sites occasionally from 1941 on, and more frequently as the invasion neared. However, much of that imagery was small-scale; good for mapping but unsuited for detailed PI work. Nor did that imagery enlarge readily to help PIs identify defenses. Of course that wasn't a serious problem until Field Marshal Rommel accelerated construction of Atlantic Wall defenses and when the Allies began planning for invasion. Then, and because of the proliferating V-Weapons threat, frequent, higher quality, better scale imagery was needed throughout the invasion area. That collection continued unabated through the invasion.

Security and bad weather forced a PR stand-down on 5 June. Heavy morning cloud cover scrubbed some PR on the 6th, but US 7 Group alone flew twenty-six missions that day, not all supporting Overlord.

I came across little coverage near H-Hour (which doesn't mean there isn't more).[14] Other than locating Airborne landings, given the time lag between imagery collection and report dissemination, PR couldn't have played much of a role on 6 June 1944. Plots indicate most of the missions were short—multiple cameras but less than 100 frames each.

To this day it's common PI practice, with a spate of coverage in a fluid ground situation, to work the newest missions first. By 1000 hours (certainly by noon even on Omaha), troops were off the beaches and moving inland so it is possible some of the mid-morning beach PR coverage was so overtaken by events that film was processed but never printed (and never looked at by busy PIs). Been there, done that. With frames of imagery rolling in faster than PIs

---

13. Fortunately the Allies had such complete command of the air that German generals could never marshal enough force to push the landing back.

14. A notable exception being the three hand-held low oblique photos starting my section on Juno. Perhaps the Canadians arranged for a C-47 flying in close because they didn't have a PR Squadron to go directly over their beaches? That cover is unique and I'd like to see more of the mission.

can scan them thoroughly the tendency is to read-out and report sortie objectives and go on to the next mission.

Afternoon imagery was reverting to the classic tactical PR role, going deeper inland, searching for enemy reinforcements, dispositions and activities out in front of the Allied advance. After the morning of 6 June, any coverage of the beaches must be considered documentary. Examples in this book from 7 June certainly were. Those missions paralleled the coast and were flown lower, returning large scale, beautifully sharp imagery (i.e., best light conditions—around noon). From mid-June on PR had a full plate supporting troop movements inland and searching France for V-1 launch sites. The beaches were covered later in June to document status of the Mulberries, and again following the big storm of 19-22 June. We see the beaches once more in early July and the last cover I found was October (a long, small scale strip covering the entire landing area). None of those PR missions were for Intelligence.

A note of caution: aerial photoreconnaissance shows events from a unique and usually enlightening perspective but from 12,000 feet war can look clean and precise—almost abstract. You see where fighting has been, seldom exactly where it was at the moment. You see little or nothing of actual contact and confusion, and nothing at all of the tension, courage, blood, noise, fear and death. Ground images and personal accounts deal with that, but they can't put what's happening in an overall context. They are flashes in time and space. They can't encompass simultaneous events. They can't freeze an entire battlefield with two or three clicks of a shutter allowing a PI to analyze the imagery (and situation) for minutes, hours, even days.

Ground shots and first-person accounts also capture a narrow context that can give a distorted impression of overall events. But first-hand accounts and photos of near disaster on Omaha are obviously the most dramatic, tending to capture the imagination and dominate public perception, skewing our understanding of the total landing operation. Every landing had to overcome initial ground fire but there was no universal experience on the beaches. The first thousand men ashore at any location faced different circumstances than soldiers landing a few miles away. Men reaching the same beach a few hours later had a yet another situation. Trapped on a beach with comrades all around being shot or blown to pieces during landing is a powerful narrative, overshadowing the fact that on other beaches other men were coming ashore relatively unscathed. A rifleman pinned down by intense machine-gun fire on Omaha couldn't imagine that east and west of him vehicles were already rolling inland bumper to bumper.

Aerial imagery tends to level all that, fostering understanding and objective analysis.

That being said, I know of no event in World War II so well covered by aerial photography as the Normandy Invasion. There are hundreds of rolls of original negatives[15] and thousands of frames to be examined to better witness and understand events in broad sweep and microcosm. I know I've only seen a fraction of that lode. Surely buried amid photos of empty fields, clouds and ocean are meaningful, even priceless, images to be identified and analyzed to select the most informative frames documenting the Invasion. What I've shown in this book is only the tip of that iceberg. It is only what I chanced to come across (and recognized as important at the time). I hope other researchers and historians will continue the work more systematically. All it takes is time, patience…and knowledge of how to look.

Photo Interpreters are not infallible, but we do see things from a different angle (no pun intended) and different time frame. I've told you what the Normandy Invasion aerial imagery I looked at said to me. If I've been successful, the reader now has a different, and more comprehensive, view of those momentous days in June 1944.

---

15. Could be up to five 500' rolls per sortie but most of these missions were 'in and outs'. Lengths were more likely less than 200' (under 200 exposures) from two or three cameras. Similar troves of RAF film are held at The Aerial Reconnaissance Archives (TARA), Glasgow, Scotland.

MAPS

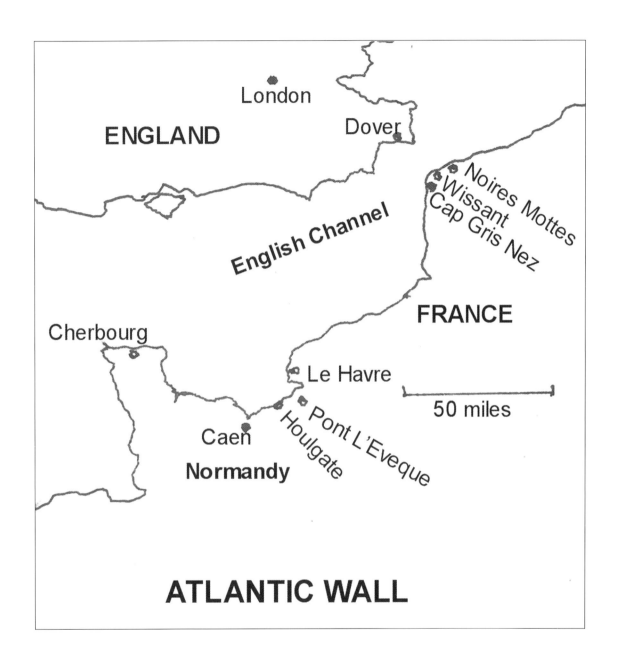

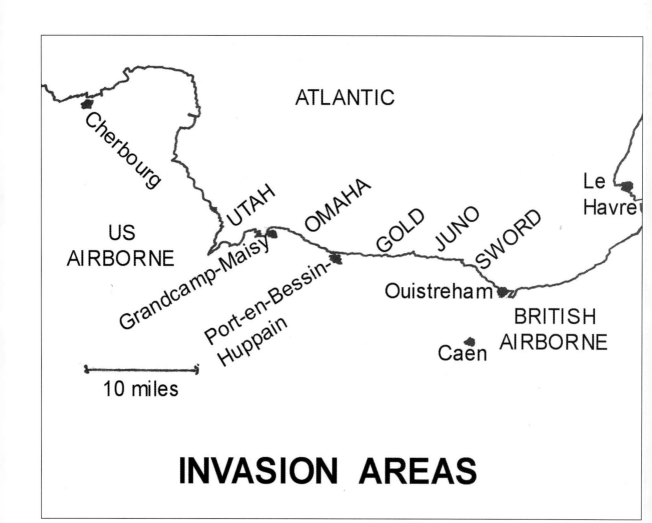

INVASION AREAS

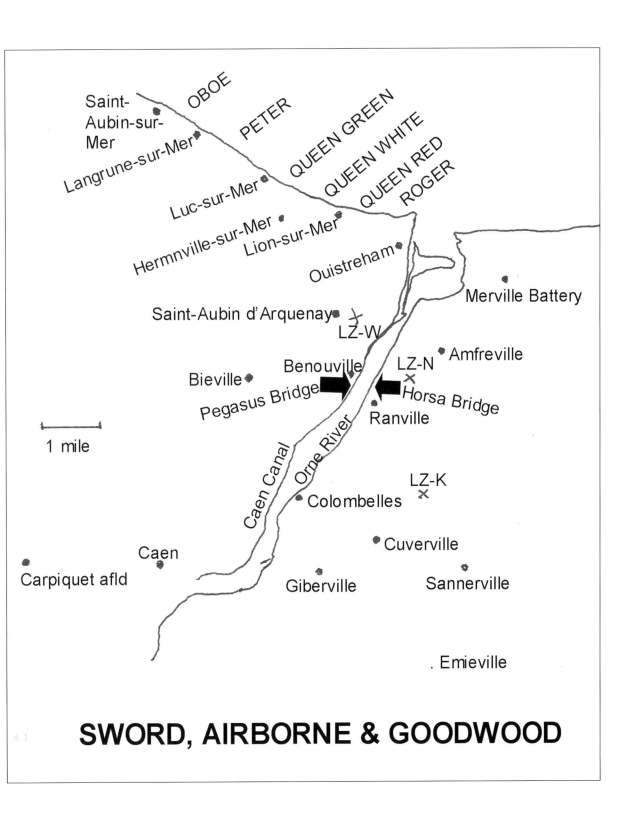

SWORD, AIRBORNE & GOODWOOD

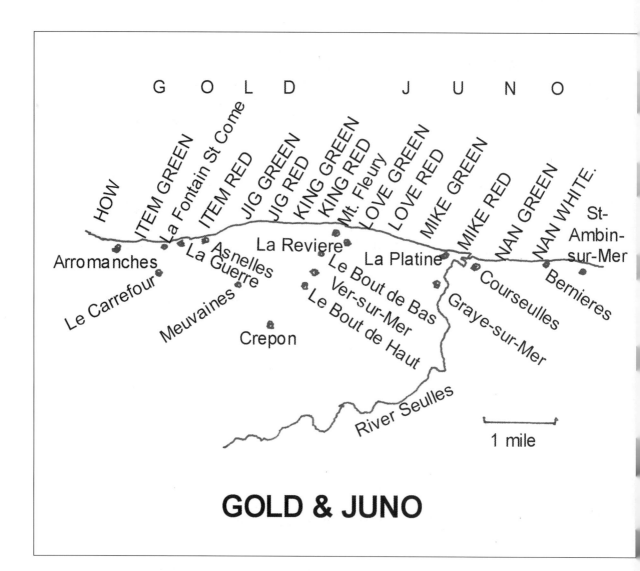

GOLD & JUNO

Pointe du Hoc

CHARLIE
DOG GREEN
DOG WHITE
DOG RED
EASY GREEN
EASY RED
FOX GREEN
FOX RED

Vierville-sur-Mer
Les Moulins Draw

Saint-Laurent-sur-Mer

Le Cavey
La Revolution

Colleville-sur-Mer

1 mile

OMAHA BEACH

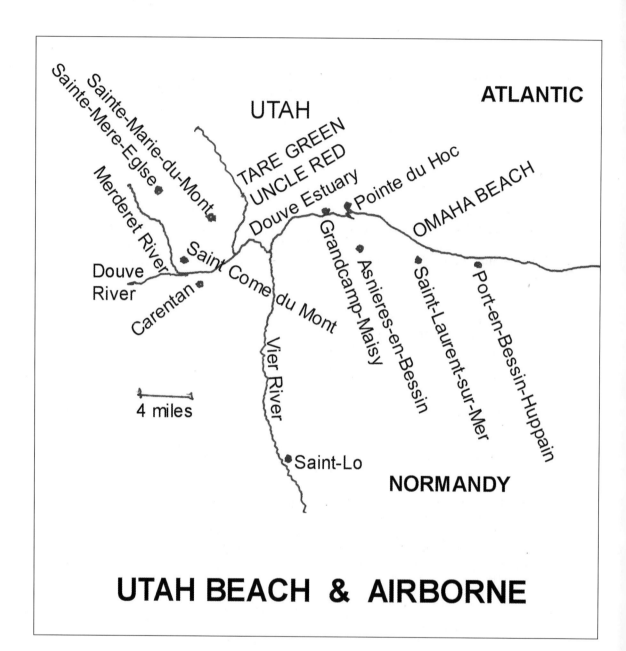

UTAH

ATLANTIC

TARE GREEN

UNCLE RED

Douve Estuary

Pointe du Hoc

OMAHA BEACH

Sainte-Marie-du-Mont

Sainte-Mere-Eglse

Merderet River

Saint Come du Mont

Grandcamp-Maisy

Asnieres-en-Bessin

Saint-Laurent-sur-Mer

Port-en-Bessin-Huppain

Douve
River

Carentan

4 miles

Vier River

Saint-Lo

NORMANDY

UTAH BEACH & AIRBORNE

INDEX

10th Photo Group (10PG) US – 40, 42

101st Airborne Div, US – 50, 75-77, 81

155mm GPF, Canon de – 17, 25, 207-210, 212-214

1st Hussars, Canadian – 108, 112

1st Infantry Div, US – 169, 180, 186, 195, 202, 254, 256, 259

21st Panzer Div, GR – 101, 112

22nd Panzer Rgt, GR – 245

29th Infantry Div, US – 169, 180, 254

2nd Ranger Bn, US – 207, 211-212, 214-215, 256

389th Bomb Group, US – 249

3rd Div, Canadian – 196

3rd Div, UK – 35, 91, 93, 100

3rd Royal Tank Rgt, UK – 246

4th Infantry Div, US – 169, 219, 220

503rd Heavy Panzer Bn, GR – 248

50th Fighter Group, US – 251

50mm anti-tank gun, GR – 13, 33, 123, 169, 172, 183, 195, 197, 199, 258

50th (Northumbrian) Inf. Div, UK – 124

6 pounder Anti-Tank gun, UK – 144, 155

6th Airborne Div, UK – 65, 69, 69f/n, 72, 85, 104

741st Armored Bn, US – 194-195

82nd Airborne Div, US – 47, 50, 63, 76, 80, 86

88mm PaK 43/41 anti-tank gun, GR – 13, 33, 100, 108, 123, 126, 169, 195, 199, 200, 258-259

8th Armored Bde, UK – 124

Advanced Landing Ground A-10 – 250-251

Amfreville – 70

Arromanches-les-Bains – 147, 160, 168-169, 238

Articulated truck – 146, 182

Asnelles – 127, 142-143, 145-146, 152, 154, 164, 167-168, 239

Asnieres-en-Bessin – 227

B-24 – 64, 67, 80, 249

Bangalore Torpedoes – 194, 257

Barrage Balloons – 91, 135, 151, 153, 175

Belgian Gates – 42, 53-54, 102, 120, 122

Benouville – 69, 69f/n, 72, 84

Bernieres-sur-Mer – 106-10, 118, 255

Bieville – 105

Bigot – 216

Bobbin tank – 99, 129, 132-133

Bocage country – 227-228, 249

Bren Gun Carrier (see Universal Carrier)

Bridging tank – 123, 179

Bulldozers – 62, 96, 99, 147, 172, 189

C-47 – 63-65, 74, 84, 86, 87, 250, 260f/n

Caen – 48, 93, 112, 122, 229, 243, 245, 246, 249, 256

Caen Canal – 19, 21, 65, 69, 69f/n, 70, 72, 84, 105, 255

Calais – 10, 12, 13, 39

Cap-Gris-Nez – 10

Carentan – 47, 76, 250

Carpiquet airfield – 229-230

Charlie, Omaha Beach – 169

Cherbourg – 17, 39, 48-49, 52, 86-87, 169, 239, 252

CLE (parachute container) – 80

Colleville-sur Mer, Draw E3 – 20, 23, 31, 189, 191-193, 195, 197-199, 205

Colombelles/Colombelles Steel Plant – 243-245

Corncobs – 232

Cotentin Peninsula – 169, 249

Courbet, FR BB – 232

Courseulles-sur-Mer – 106, 108, 117, 119-120, 122, 255,

Crab (see flail tank)

Crepon – 162

Cuverville – 244

Czech Hedgehogs – 40-41, 43, 45, 57-58, 96, 100, 102, 119-121, 138, 173, 177

DD M4 tank (see M4)

Dog Green, Omaha Beach – 169

Dog Red, Omaha Beach – 22, 29, 171, 197

Douve River/Estuary – 74, 216, 218,224, 227

Dover, UK – 10

DUKW amphibious truck – 116, 122, 136, 169, 173, 182

East Yorkshire Rgt, UK – 98

Easy Green, Omaha Beach – 22, 29, 171, 173-174, 176, 197

Easy Red, Omaha Beach – 23, 31, 174, 177, 179-180, 186, 193-194, 196, 255

Emieville – 246

English Channel – 11, 63, 69

F-5 (see P-38)

Flail Tank – 61-62, 93, 97, 155

Fort Garry Horse, Canadian – 112

Fox, Omaha Beach – 23, 31, 169, 192, 195-196, 201-202, 205, 255

Giberville – 244

Gleaves-class DD, US – 192

Gooseberry – 189, 223, 231-232, 236, 242

Grandcamp-Maisy – 169, 209, 212

Graye-sur-Mer – 117

Green Howards Rgt, UK – 141

Hamilcar glider – 73, 81

Hermanville-sur-Mer – 94

Higgins Boat – 68, 136, 148, 182, 193, 201, 203, 216, 219, 231, 241

HMS *Belfast* – 141

HMS *Durban* – 232

HNLMS *Sumatra* – 282

Hobart's Funnies – 61, 96-97, 123

Horsa Bridge – 21, 69f/n

Horsa glider – 64-65, 69, 73, 78-79, 81-84, 87

Houlgate – 26

How, Gold Beach – 124

Isle of Wight, UK – 239

Item Red, Gold Beach – 167-168

Jig Green, Gold Beach – 145-148, 151, 154, 167

Jig Red, Gold Beach – 143, 156, 164

Ju 52 – 229

King Green, Gold Beach – 127, 130-131, 134-135, 137-138, 142-143, 158, 162

King Red, Gold Beach – 125-128

La Fontaine Saint-Come – 168-169, 241

La Guerre – 168

La Madeleine – 217

La Platine – 117

La Revolution, Draw F1 – 20, 23, 31, 169, 201, 203, 206

La Sapiniere – 20, 180

Landing Zone "N" – 70

Landing Zone "W" – 85

LCA (Landing Craft Assault) – 68, 92, 109, 139, 148, 231

LCI (Landing Craft Infantry) – 91-92, 95, 116, 178, 186

LCM (Landing Craft Mechanized) – 120-121

LCT (Landing Craft Tank) – 91-92, 95, 100, 108-110, 116, 120, 124, 133-136, 139, 146, 149, 152, 165, 169, 177-178, 193, 195, 203-206

Le Bout-de-Bas – 127, 142

Le Bout-de-Haut – 143-144, 156

Le Carrefour – 160

Le Cavey – 20, 31, 195, 199

Le Hamel – 127, 155

Le Havre – 17, 169, 253

Les Moulins, Draw D3 – 20, 22, 29, 43-44, 89, 171, 176, 255-256

Lindemann Battery – 12

Lion-sur-Mer – 97, 100, 102

Love, Juno Beach – 106

LST (Landing Ship Tank) – 103-104, 253

Luc-sur-Mer – 112, 122

M4 "Sherman" tank – 61, 91, 97, 108-109, 111-112, 123, 129-130, 132-133, 166, 169, 172, 183, 193-195, 204, 219, 258-259

M7 "Priest" 105mm SP – 180

Medmenham – 6, 207, 211

Merderet River – 74, 76

Merville Battery/Merville – 21, 70-71

Meuvaines – 157-158, 160, 162-163

Mike Green, Juno Beach – 108, 117

Mike Red, Juno Beach – 108, 119

Mines/Minefields – 13, 16, 18, 41, 49, 52, 56, 58-59, 61, 90, 97, 100, 126, 141-144, 146, 155, 158-159, 172-173, 183, 252, 256

Mont Fleury (La Riviere) – 125-127, 131, 134, 143, 151, 255

Mont Fleury Battery – 140-142, 156, 158-159, 209, 257, 259

Mulberry A – 170, 190, 237, 239, 242

Mulberry B – 237-240

Nan Green, Juno Beach – 107, 113-114, 122

Nan White, Juno Beach – 107, 109, 115

Neger, GR manned torpedo – 232

Noires Mottes Battery – 12

Oboe, Sword Beach – 91

Omaha Beach – 20, 22-24, 29-31, 45, 52, 57, 89, 129, 147, 169-208, 227, 236-237 242, 254-261

Operation Goodwood – 243, 246-248

Operation Husky – 63

Operation Neptune – 63-64

Operation Overlord – 19, 62-63, 107, 208-209, 212, 226, 235, 254, 260

Orne River – 19, 21, 35-36, 69f/n, 70, 72, 74, 85, 88, 93, 243

Ouistreham – 19, 35, 85, 91, 231, 252

P-38/F-5 – 33, 41-42, 66-67, 78, 192, 218

P-47 – 66, 251-252

Pegasus Bridge – 69f/n, 84, 86, 104

Peter, Sword Beach - 91

Phoenix breakwater segment – 46

PLUTO (Pipe-Lines Under The Ocean) – 239

Pointe du Hoc – 28, 207-216, 256

Porpoise sledge – 93

Port-en-Bessin-Huppain – 147, 255

Pyramids, beach defense – 39, 41, 55-56, 58-60

Quaker guns – 212

Queen Green, Sword Beach – 92-94, 97, 100

Queen Red, Sword Beach – 32-33, 98-99, 103, 231

Queen White, Sword Beach – 32, 91-92, 95, 103, 231

Ramps, beach defense – 41, 43, 45, 59, 60, 100, 173, 177-178

Ranville – 69f/n, 70, 72-73, 88

Regina Rifles, Canadian – 108

Rhino Ferries – 119, 122, 136, 177, 206, 223, 236

Roger, Sword Beach – 32, 34-36, 91, 256

Rommel Asparagus – 48-49, 65, 71, 73, 141

Rommel, Field Marshall Erwin, GR – 13, 16, 52, 209-210

Rommelspargel (see Rommel Asparagus)

Saint-Aubin d'Arquenay – 84

Saint-Aubin-sur-Mer – 91, 106

Sainte-Marie-du-Mont – 75, 77, 81

Sainte-Mere-Eglise – 47, 76, 81, 86

Saint-Laurent-sur-Mer, Draw E1 – 20, 30, 45, 146, 169-170, 174, 179-186, 189-193, 202

Saint-Lo – 249

Sannerville – 246

Seulles River – 117, 119

Sherman (see M4)

Strong points – 8, 12-14, 32-33, 90, 98, 106-108, 121, 168-169, 171-172, 180, 184, 188, 191, 193, 198, 102, 255-256, 259-260

Swimming Tank (see M4)

Tare Green, Utah Beach – 49, 216, 223

Teller Mines – 49, 56

Todt Battery, organization – 10-12

Uncle Red, Utah Beach – 50, 224

Universal Carrier – 83, 94, 113, 144, 155-157

USS Corry – 192

V-1, flying bomb – 7, 72, 210, 213, 232, 281

Ver-sur-Mer – 143, 156, 158

Vierville-sur Mer, Draw D1 – 20, 42, 169-170, 255

Vire River – 169

Waco glider – 63-65, 74-75, 77, 79, 81-82, 86-87

Wading tank (see M4)

Widerstandsnest (see strong points)

Wissant – 10-11